Playtime for Cats

Activities and games for felines

by Stefanie Sigl and Helena Dbalý

Copyright © 2008 by Cadmos Verlag GmbH, Brunsbek
Copyright of this edition © 2009 by Cadmos Books, Great Britain
Translated by Andrea Höfling
Title Photograph: Tierfotoagentur/Ramona Richter
Layout: Ravenstein + Partner, Verden
Photographs: animal digital/Thomas Brodmann,
Helena Dbalý, Christiane Slawik, Tierfotoagentur/Ramona Richter
Editorial: Anneke Bosse
Editorial of this edition: Dr. Sarah Binns, Christopher Long
Printed by: Westermann Druck, Zwickau

British Library Cataloguing in Publication Data
A catalogue record of this book is available from the British Library.

Printed in Germany

ISBN 978-3-86127-970-9

Playtime
for Cats

Contents

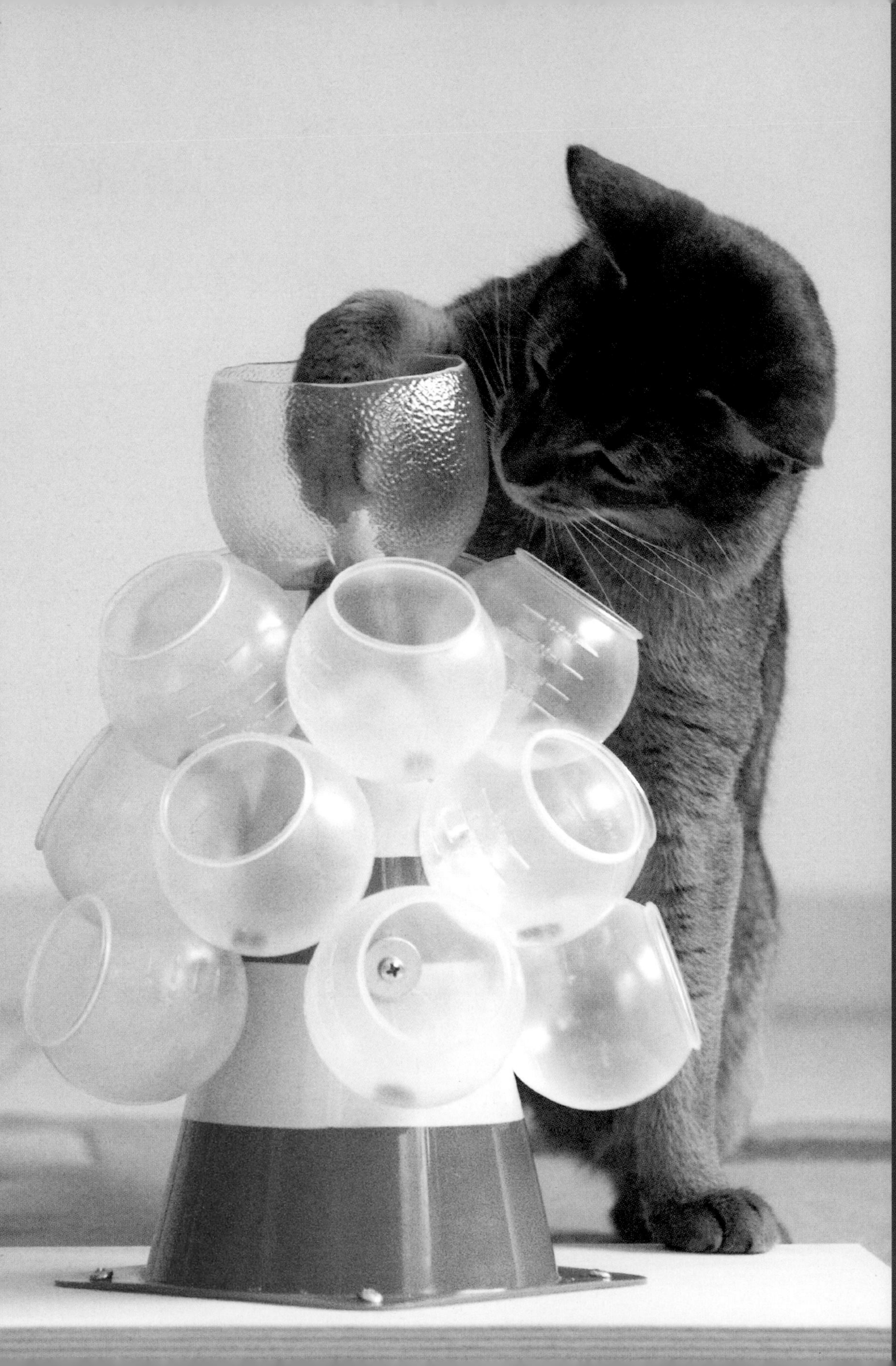

(Photo: Slawik)

Contents

Thank you!

We are particularly grateful to Birgit Laser who laid the foundations for the creation of this book. We would also like to thank all the photographers for their lovely photos, in particular Christine Slawik who has taken beautiful pictures of cats in the Anja Pignataro's 'Katzehuus' in Pratteln (CH) and in the private home of Cornelia Brägger in a happy and relaxed atmosphere.

We owe huge praise to our four-legged cat models, who patiently and with enthusiasm and stamina cooperated in our photo shoots.

We would like to thank Elin Grammenthaler (aged 16) and Rena Schenke (aged 7) for the lovely photo opportunities they provided while playing with their feline friends Faramir and Plato.

We would also like to thank Dr Kurt Neeser for his critical review of the chapter about the fumbling board for cats and his constructive suggestions.

Finally we would like to thank our proofreader, Anneka Bosse, for her unstinting cooperation.

Stefanie Sigl and
Helena Dbaly

(Rolf: many heartfelt thanks for your never-ending patience during the creation of this book.)

What's the point of a book on games for cats?

because cats need to play to live!

Scientifically speaking, playing is fun-based experimentation with motivated behaviour without the real life relevance typical of such behaviours. To a cat, play means simply having fun – the fun of movement, social interaction, and looking for things, ambushing them and catching them.

Kittens explore their environment through play. They learn correct social behaviour by playing with their mother and littermates. They also experience their own body during play, and how it moves. They also learn, playfully, what kind of strategy to employ to skilfully catch particular prey. To put it briefly, playing means 'learning for life'.

Just like human beings, cats change their play behaviour during the course of their lives. Young cats want to run wild and try out their hunting skills. Adult cats no longer have the same urge to move as do kittens. For the hunt they rely more on experience, skill and cunning. As a result, adult cats enjoy brain-teasers and strategy games for which young cats often do not have sufficient patience.

Cats can reach a ripe old age if well looked after. In all likelihood they'll be suffering from any number of small ailments by then, and every step needs to be carefully considered. Their sense of hearing and their eyesight are also in decline. These cat pensioners would have long ago given up catching prey out of doors. But a stone that doesn't move gathers moss. Usually these cats are still mentally alert, the old bones are still mobile, and the eyes are still keen enough to 'kill' stationary prey. Given the choice, most cat pensioners would reject a well-filled food bowl and instead turn to food that they can fumble and paw out of holes and crevices or unwrap from a parcel. Many old cats are very grateful even for brief playing sessions where the main emphasis is on the social contact with the human being who has been with them all their lives.

For indoor cats playing is of particular importance. Indoor cats can express their natural behaviours only in a very limited way. They lack the opportunity to roam in a manner appropriate for their species in order to hunt and to react to diverse environmental stimuli. If their humans don't offer them the necessary stimuli to help them to express their natural behaviours, they can develop behavioural problems. Varied and exciting play can prevent this from happening, and thus deepen the relationship with their human. Play-based therapy can help solve the problems of cats with behavioural difficulties.

Like all highly evolved beings, cats have a life-long urge to play. If a cat doesn't play (any more) this may be a serious warning sign. Either the cat's life circumstances have led to the loss of his or her zest for life, and with it for play, or the cat may be seriously ill.

(Photo: Slawik)

Rules of play
for human and cat

To enable both humans and cats to enjoy this book, there are some issues that need to be borne in mind:

🐾 Cats love rituals and ordered daily routines – and hence fixed play times.

🐾 Toys that are always available quickly lose their attraction. You should always tidy away any toys after use. Turn the time you spend playing with your cat into a special moment in their daily routine, it will strengthen the bond between you.

🐾 When choosing toys for your cat take your cue from the natural variety of prey available to cats. Cats predominantly catch insects, mice, small reptiles and small song-birds. A mouse is about the size of a thumb. Many toys are significantly larger, and therefore of no interest whatsoever to your cat. It is even possible that your cat will be scared of toys that are too large.

Please also make sure that the toys you buy are well made. Sharp edges, loose wire, and threads hanging loose have no place on a cat toy. Please also remove glued-on plastic parts from any toy before play. If the cat were to tear off and swallow such parts this may cause serious health problems.

To be adapted to the cat's activity rhythms a playing session should last between fifteen and thirty minutes. Don't worry – this doesn't mean that you have to drag a bunch of feathers behind you on a string for half an hour. A game with the bunch of feathers, which the cat will alternately ambush and catch, can develop into a 'find the food' game, and end with your cat fishing for prey from a cardboard box.

Cats only do things if they are worth their while, therefore you should allow your cat to win any hunting games. They quickly lose interest in a game at which they are unsuccessful.

Design all new games so they can be easily learned by the cat. Cats are very prone to getting frustrated. They need quick successes to prevent them from throwing in the towel.

Take regular breaks and make sure the cat doesn't get overexcited. Cats are not pack hunters who chase their prey. Movement alternates with concentrated waiting for the right moment to pounce. It may look cute when a kitten chases after a dot of light for minutes on end, zigzagging and tripping over his own legs. Please bear in mind, however, that Mother Nature has not equipped cats for this form of hunting. In nature the prey would either have been caught, have flown away, have disappeared into a hole, or become rigid long since.

Let boisterous play end on a calm note. Draw the cat's attention to something that requires their full concentration. This will help guide their energy slowly into calmer waters.

Make sure you vary the games you play. Cats aren't just good at moving. They are also highly intelligent animals who need to occupy their minds.

Take your cue from the cat when deciding what kind of game to play. A free-roaming cat who can exercise the urge to move out of doors doesn't need to be exercised at home as well. Young cats play in a different way from OAPs. Single cats have different needs for play and social contact from those of cats who live with other cats. A tomcat's behaviour is different from that of a female cat. Watch your cats – they will show you which games they like.

Cats are hunters, but in their natural environment they themselves are also hunted. They are very jumpy and quickly take flight. Therefore avoid making unnecessary noise around your cat, and don't scare a cat by making sudden, quick movements. Try to stay on the same level as your cat during play, or stay at a distance. Compared with a cat you are a giant who can easily appear threatening.

• Don't ever use your hands and fingers as prey. Draw the cat's interest towards suitable objects. This way you'll avoid your cat considering your hands as prey from the very beginning. Should your cat already be a ruffian, break off any play as soon as the cat displays rough behaviour. Interrupting play and an audible 'ouch' will teach the cat that this kind of behaviour is not worthwhile. As soon as the cat has calmed down you can continue playing.

• Even if it's difficult, keep your head. If a cat sinks their claws into your arm, keep perfectly still. The less you struggle, the sooner the cat will let go. Resistance encourages a cat to tighten their grip, and to struggle with the prey or adversary (at this moment in time that's what your arm is to the cat). This can cause serious injuries.

• If your cat isn't interested in playing as much as usual, bear in mind that he or she may be in pain, or possibly sick.

• If a cat that has only recently moved in doesn't want to play, they are probably scared. Allow sufficient time for the cat to familiarise themselves with their new surroundings and to build up trust. Try your luck from a distance, or give the cat games they can play while undisturbed on their own (and also at night).

• If you have more than one cat, make sure that all your cats get equal amounts of attention. If necessary you can play with each cat separately, one after the other.

Smelltastic –
smells, herbs, catnip, valerian, etc.

Drugs for cats?

A cat's nasal lining is twice as large, in relative terms, and has ten to twenty times as many olfactory cells, as a human's – this astonishing comparison gives us some idea of how hugely important the sense of smell must be for cats.

There are particular smells that will put some cats into rather 'high spirits' (although without a hangover the next day). The cat will rub against the odoriferous object, gnaw it and drool over it with an expression of rapture, getting more and more ecstatic.

Toys that have been scented with attractively smelling substances can cause cats to burst into fits of ecstasy. (Photo: Dbalý)

This 'trip' will normally last for about fifteen minutes. A note of caution: some cats can be irritable and aggressive during this period. To be on the safe side, they should be left alone for a few minutes after they've come down from the 'high' – otherwise a quick blow with a paw might be coming your way. The most well known cat 'drug' is catnip. However, valerian and the wood from lonicera may also lead to a state of intoxication in many cats. Be careful: the leaves of lonicera are toxic. Furthermore, some cats may have very individual predilections for certain herbs and vegetables.

Tomcat Timmy becomes totally entranced upon smelling root vegetables or soup herbs on his owner's fingers. Little Pauline, on the other hand, prefers the smell of sage.

Catnip can be obtained as a dried herb or as a pre-prepared mixture with a variety of other herbs from a pet shop. You can also buy the smelling agents of catnip and lonicera as a spray, while valerian is available from any pharmacy as a tincture that can be dripped on to toys or small fabric bags. If you have a garden or a balcony you can of course also grow catnip yourself. If you want to keep these smells special for your cat, make sure you prevent your cat from having constant access to your herb patch.

Scented toys

Ready-made little fabric bags filled with catnip and lonicera are available from pet shops. Make sure they are still wrapped in airtight packaging at the time of purchase. If you like, you can also make scented toys yourself. Using a spray or a tincture you can add some fragrance to any toy you may have in the house. Use all scents very sparingly, however. A cat's sense of smell is far more pronounced than ours. One drop of valerian tincture, or a single burst of catnip spray, is quite sufficient. You can also put furry balls or toy mice in a jar filled with dried catnip for a while. They absorb the smell easily.

You'll notice that the cat isn't playing with the scented toy in the usual manner, hunting and catching it. The cat would rather bite into it and rub against it.

An old cloth with drops of valerian tincture on it, or sprayed with catnip, fulfils the same purpose as commercially available toys and has the advantage that it is washable. Because cats tend to drool profusely during these ecstatic fits the scented toys will soon become unsightly.

Pressed cotton wool balls the size of table tennis balls are available from craft shops and can be scented at home to provide a special experience for your cat. Cats are not just able to rub against these balls; they can drench them with gusto, bite into them and rip them apart. Should you notice your cat eating the cotton wool, a ball made from scrunched-up newspaper can provide an alternative.

For tomcat Faramir his humans' laundry is so exciting that he will rub against it. (Photo: Dbalý)

A punchbag for scallywags

Some cats don't just roll around in the catnip, valerian, etc. They will also start fighting with the scented items. Just like in (playful) 'contra-toms' with other cats they lie on their side or on their back, hold on to the scented item with their front paws and pound it with their hind paws. If you have a little fighter like that at home, give him a punchbag as a sparring partner. A tomcat can really work off his aggression on a woollen sock that has been fragranced with his favourite smell.

There are some cats – they tend usually to be toms – who will scare fellow cats by their very physical way of playing. The punchbag provides a good opportunity for such a scallywag to exercise his need for fighting and scrapping without terrorising the neighbourhood.

For all designated toys the rule is that they should not be available all the time. This should apply especially to scented toys. Although these brief moments of intoxication represent no risk to the cat, they should remain special. Apart from that, even the nicest smelling scented toy loses its attraction if the cat can smell it all the time.

What's the rascal doing in my laundry?

It is not just the smell of certain plants and herbs that can make cats ecstatic. Smells are of particular importance for the social life of cats. A large part of inter-feline communication happens via 'scented messages'. All cats deposit olfactory substances (pheromones) on objects and on social partners, when they spray urine or rub their chin against them. All cats are also very interested in the scented messages of other cats. They will investigate spots where other cats have sat, scratched or rubbed against. However, it is not only the social smells of other cats that are worth investigating. We humans also emit pheromones, and some cats crave these human smells.

They don't just love the worn pyjamas or nighties of their owners. Every item of clothing that has been worn close to the body will put these cats into fits of delight. They stick their nose and mouth deeply into the fabric and suck in air; this is known as the gape or flehmen response.

What is the gape or flehmen response?

'Flehmen' means that a cat sucks in certain smells through the open mouth. The olfactory substances stream through two little holes behind the front teeth and into the vomeronasal organ. There they provide important information about the identity of the smell and its originator. A cat showing a flehmen response sits with its head tilted backwards while drawing back the upper lip.

Very few people leave their dirty laundry lying around in their house. Tidy as we are, we put it into the laundry basket and from there into the washing machine. By doing this we potentially prevent our cats from partaking in a great olfactory pleasure. So why not let the cat have a go at the open sports bag after you come home from the gym, or the laundry basket on laundry day, in order to allow them an olfactory experience of a special kind every now and then?

(Photo: Richter)

A mouse,
a mouse!

You have probably seen cats who, instead of eating their prey, throw it around, let it escape, catch it again and play with it. This hunting behaviour displayed by cats has been disconnected from the feeling of hunger.

Free-roaming cats who are fed by humans, and hence rarely experience hunger, are just as successful at hunting as cats who have to provide for themselves.

Cats have a reflex reaction to certain movements and noises, and look specifically for situations that trigger hunting behaviour. If they live in a flat, or where there is only limited opportunity to roam, it is very important that their human provides the necessary stimuli through play.

The play behaviour of cats is moulded by the behaviour that they display during hunting.

When, how and what do cats hunt?

The question of when cats hunt can be answered quickly: whenever they're awake and the relevant stimuli are in place that prompt them to react. Possible triggers are quiet cheeping, rustling and scratching noises, as well as quick jerky movements, especially movements that are moving away from the cat's field of vision.

A cat's natural spectrum of potential prey includes insects, mice and other small rodents, small reptiles such as lizards and grass snakes, songbirds, fish and in rare cases large rats, fully grown rabbits and other small game. They usually only play with smaller prey animals, such as mice, that are not dangerous. Insects such as grasshoppers and flies are rarely eaten, and most cats do not eat them at all. Cats busy themselves with their prey; they paw it, nudge it, let it get away again and again, and then catch it again. When choosing cat toys you would be well advised to take your cue from nature and to choose toys that are reminiscent of the real thing in size, shape and the way they move.

This cat catches a fabric toy mouse in the living room with as much enthusiasm as he would any live prey outside. (Photo: Richter)

Commercially available toys

Play can contain all the elements of a hunting sequence, i.e. ambushing the prey, sneaking up on it, pouncing on it, catching it in the mouth and/or with the front paws, letting it go and allowing it to escape, throwing it in the air and catching it again, pawing it out of crevices and holes, carrying it off and hiding it, in all possible combinations.

You can spend huge amounts of money on toys on the Internet or in pet shops. Many of these toys are too large and too unwieldy to appeal to cats, others are so badly made that they are outright dangerous. However, there are also well designed and sensible toys available that will provide a lot of fun for you and your cat.

The young tomcat Plato still fits inside the circle and doesn't have to walk around on the outside. (Photo: Slawik)

Magic roundabout

A roundabout for cats is one of the few commercially available toys that cats can play with on their own for relatively long periods of time. It consists of two round halves, which form a pipe circle that is open on the outside. There are usually also a few openings on the top. Inside the pipe is a ball. Show your cat that the ball can move inside the pipe – they will be fascinated watching the ball going round and round. The cat will walk around the roundabout and carefully touch the ball with its paws.

The cat quickly learns how to put on the brakes or speed the ball up. Now nothing can stand in the way of an exhilarating chase. Roundabouts for cats are available in a variety of versions and from different brands. Make sure that the roundabout is well made. The mouse, which is often fixed on a spring in the middle, should be removed for safety reasons. Cats may get their fur pinched in the spring or hurt themselves should the mouse come off.

Fabric mice and furry balls

Cats tend to be very enthusiastic about furry balls and fabric mice; they are not just able to nudge them with their paws and run them across the room like a penalty zone dribbler. The soft material enables the cat to pick up the toy with their claws, throw it around and catch it again. They can also carry it around just like a real mouse.

Cats play differently with balls from the way they play with mice. Some need a little encouragement, by way of the human throwing the toy once, in order to delve subsequently into a play world of their own. Other cats need a playing partner, who will throw or roll the prey for them time and again, and then they will tear after it and catch it. Owners of cats who can 'fetch' are lucky indeed!

Some cats develop a game that involves them and their human taking turns throwing balls to each other. Just like a goalkeeper during training, they wait for the ball, catch it in mid-air and hurl it back.

Many cats take hold of toy mice by the tail, and carry them hanging halfway out of their mouths.
(Photo: Slawik)

For the agile prey on the end of the dangling rod most cats will literally leap into the air.
(Photo: Dbalý)

The dangling rod

A dangling rod is a plastic rod that has various objects dangling from it on a piece of string or an elastic band, such as fabric mice, strips of leather, small feather boas or other items. Make sure that the toy is not too bulky. If in doubt choose the smallest, lightest and most delicate item. Dangling rods with feather boas usually prove particularly irresistible to cats.

With a dangling rod for cats you can play on the ground and in the air. Just drag the rod behind you, letting it stop ever so often, and let the prey jump about in leaps and bounds. Move it in the same way as an actual mouse or a bird would move, and you will be guaranteed to get your cat's full attention. The cat will sneak up on it, look for cover, pursue the prey, and at some point pounce and grab it in one leap. A note of caution: as soon as the cat has caught the prey and holds on to it, the elastic band will become taut. Whatever you do, don't let go of the rod now. Move the rod towards the cat and try to release the tension on the elastic band, because the cat may suddenly let go as well. This toy can literally have your eye out.

You can play with the dangling rod while sitting down; you can, however, also lure the cat across the whole house, up the scratching tree, and over chairs and tables and cupboards. Just make sure the rod makes small jerky movements, and let it stop every so often in between. Cats find prey that can no longer be seen particularly interesting. Let the prey on the end of the rod quickly disappear behind the door frame, under the rug or duvet, or behind the sofa cushion.

The feather play rod

The feather play rod has feathers or leather strips attached directly to the tip of a plastic rod. If you move this rod through the air a slight distance away, the cat will try and bash it, and try to catch the birdie.

Feather play rods are very well suited for playing with timid cats who don't normally play in the presence of humans, and who are scared of the wide ranging movements that play with the dangling rod involves. When a cat is sitting on the scratching tree or another elevated spot while observing the surrounding area, carefully approach in a way, preferably from the side, that makes you seem less of a threat. As you're getting closer, make yourself seem smaller. Sit down on the

floor or a chair that you have put there beforehand, and play your way from the ground upwards towards the cat. Move the feather play rod sideways and up and down around the edge of the area where the cat is sitting. This way the cat can see only your arm, giving you a less threatening and inhibiting appearance, and thus enabling the cat to enjoy playing even more.

With the feather play rod even timid cats can quickly be encouraged to play. (Photo: Slawik)

The CatDancer®

For timid cats, the CatDancer® can also be a wonderful plaything. This unassuming looking toy from the USA consists of a bouncy piece of wire that has a number of small paper twists attached to it. If you hold the wire loosely between your fingers, it bounces up and down and sideways, making the paper twists dance in the air like insects.

Human-orientated cats are enthusiastic about the CatDancer® too. You'll be surprised to see the aerobatics and jumps your cats will perform as soon as they try to catch those paper twists. Unfortunately the CatDancer® is difficult to obtain from retailers. You can, however, get it via the Internet relatively easily.

The laser pointer

We are no great friends of laser pointers, because they offer the cat no sense of success. Even if the cat does catch the light, they won't have anything in their paws. In most cases the laser pointer is used in a way that sends the cat running after it in wild goose chase back and forth, making the cat very agitated both physically and mentally. After a few minutes spent running after the laser pointer, most cats get overexcited and frustrated.

This is not a constructive way to occupy your cat. In addition there is a risk of causing eye injury. For some cats who are predisposed, there is the additional danger that they may begin to chase other light spots, e.g. those produced by sunlight. This may lead to stereotypy, i.e. obsessive behaviours that may in the worst case result in self-inflicted injury.

However, especially when dealing with timid cats who cannot be reached through normal play, play with the laser pointer can be deployed usefully as an occupational tool. The laser pointer enables you to act and arouse the cat's interest from a great distance without at the same time inhibiting them. Make the light spot rush

The small bouncing paper twists have a magical attraction for cats. (Photo: Dbalý)

back and forth, hold it still for a moment, before letting it disappear behind the leg of a chair … in short, try to make the light spot move like a mouse. As soon as the cat takes up the pursuit, use the laser pointer merely as a signpost to direct the cat towards bits of food laid out beforehand, or to bags of catnip or furry mice. When combined with such hunting successes for the cat the laser pointer can be a very amusing toy for cat and human alike.

You can also use a torch as an alternative. Lasers and LEDs project small light spots, often no larger than a coin. Many cats are easily encouraged to play by the larger light spots produced by a torch. Of course, torches are also not supposed to be used just to make the cat chase madly around the place.

Home-made toys

You don't have to buy toys in order to present your cat with a multitude of ideas for playthings. You can quite easily put your own ideas for things to play with into practice, which will be enjoyed just as much by you and your cat.

Household items

Drinking straws, pens, plastic bottle lids, wine corks, the cut off corners from tetra packs, crunched up tin foil, hair elastics, table tennis balls … some of these items can probably be found in your household. If your cat hasn't shown you long ago what fantastic toys you have in your house, take another look at the items you handle every day, and see them through a cat's eyes. Everything light and small enough to be moved by a cat's paw,

This tom has a weakness for pasta twirls …

… balls made from tin foil …

… and hair elastics.
(Photos: Slawik)

but too large for kitty to swallow, is a suitable toy that the cat can play with happily on their own for a period of time.

Supposedly there are collectors among cats, who squirrel away various treasures such as uncooked pasta twirls, cable binders and similar loot to a secret hiding place. If things go missing on a regular basis in your house, ask kitty …

Paper aeroplanes

If you have a child – or even a grown-up – in your household who is able to fold paper aeroplanes, ask him or her to build a glider. From a chair the children can gently send the glider on its journey. If the glider really does glide calmly and doesn't start spiralling out of control, it may also be suitable as a transporter for tasty treats.

Catching beer mats

Next time you go to the pub, take a beer mat home for your cat. They too can fly, if you throw them like a frisbee. And – which is substantially more important as far as cats are concerned – you can roll them. With a bit of dexterity you will quickly learn how to roll the disc in a straight line or in a curve, and your cat will happily run along next to it. Some cats will stop the beer mat with their paw or mouth, and subsequently tear it to pieces. Others wait until the mats fall over by themselves, and then fetch and guard them. If your cat is less destructively inclined than some, you can also use coasters made from cork.

Playing with string

Most cats can never get enough of pieces of string snaking across the floor. A play rod is more suitable for when you're sitting, or standing still. However, if you're walking around, your cat will be enormously pleased if you're dragging a piece of string behind you. Just bear in mind that play objects are of most interest to cats when they are moving out of the field of vision. A piece of string disappearing around the door frame must be pursued without delay.

This kind of game can very easily be integrated into everyday routines. Tie a piece of string to your ankle and carry out those household tasks that require you to walk around. The cat will be excited by this indoor snake, and will ambush it as soon as it stays still for a moment, and leap after it in a mad pursuit once it disappears around the corner, to catch it and let it go again and again.

Please don't leave the pieces of string lying around the place after finishing play because they could be dangerous if the cat were to eat them.

Catching food

A surprisingly easy method to keep cats occupied while you are for example watching television or reading consists of throwing dried cat food to the side. Cats just love running after the munchies on the floor, catching them and eating them.

This game can be played with varying degrees of difficulty for the cat as well as the human. Try aiming to throw the food inside a cardboard or a plastic box. The cat has to leap after it into the box in order to get the treat. If the cat stays inside the box, throw the next piece somewhere else in the room, forcing the cat to jump out of the box again. You can fill the box with various objects in order to make the search a little more demanding for the cat.

For this you can use plastic balls, for example, or pine cones, corks or scrunched-up newspaper. Now the cat has to use their nose as well, in order to discover the treat.

Beware of too much extra food

Please make sure that you deduct the amount of food that you use for playing from the cat's daily food rations. Cats get noticeably plumper around the hips over time after being given just one extra heaped tablespoon of dried cat food every day.

Some manufacturers produce their dried food in very large lumps. If you halve these using a tablet-splitting device from a pharmacy your cat will get to have twice the fun.

When you have mastered aiming the treats inside a box, try your luck with more difficult targets. Are you able to hit the seat of a stool or a chair, and in such a way that the treat doesn't fall off again? This game is a good starting point for training the use of a signal for the cat to come to you. There is more about this subject in the chapter on training a cat, on page 56.

Catching food is an especially suitable game for fat cats. Such cats are often not particularly interested in playing games, but if food is involved, they are often prepared to walk a few steps. Take advantage of this opportunity by making your cat work for their food. Even if your little roly-poly likes playing, have them earn their food anyway. If you do that you can even reduce the rations, because if a cat has to catch its own food, it will spend a lot more time eating its meals than if the food bowl is just put in front of it. The cat won't even be aware that it is getting less food. As a side effect the cat is also having fun, getting a sense of success, and, on top of that, self-caught food just tastes so much nicer.

If you are not feeding dried cat food, in the next chapter you'll find ideas for how to build different foods into a food obstacle course for cats.

Going after the treat with gusto in a box filled with plastic eggs and champagne corks.
(Photo: Slawik)

For the curious cat – searching and unwrapping

Almost all the aforementioned toys and ideas for play have something in common. Their object consists mainly of pursuing and catching, and they are only fun when the human joins in and moves the toys around. For playtime ideas that take advantage of the proverbial curiosity of cats, they don't need a playing partner. The human needs only to make a few preparations, and then lean back and watch his or her cat play at leisure.

Searching for food

You have probably observed many times before how your cat makes patrol rounds through the house in order to check that everything is in order? Prepare a few surprises by leaving various treats for your cat to find on their rounds. Dried food is particularly suitable for this purpose. In order to get your cat to develop a taste for this game and to stimulate their enthusiasm for the search, you can initially deploy different and particularly tasty treats. You can place any food that may leave a stain on small saucers, coasters or the lids of jam jars turned upside down.

Please don't forget to deduct the treats used in any of the games in this chapter from your cat's daily rations.

Suitable hiding places are on the scratching tree, on the windowsills, on top of and inside cupboards, underneath and behind furniture, behind doors and between flowerpots. You will know where the best hiding places are in your house.

At the beginning make it as easy as possible for your cat, and show them that you are laying out food for them. While the cat is eating the first munchies on the window sill, move on and put a piece of food between two flowerpots. The cat will watch you and follow you immediately. This way you leave treats in different places with the cat in close pursuit. The next time the cat will probably already know what you're up to and you can speed up the laying out of treats, while still using the same spots as the first time. The cat has remembered them and will check the exact places. You can increase the challenge every time, add new spots in which to leave food and extend your rounds to include more rooms.

The point of this food search game is that the cat is made to wait outside, or in another room, while you lay out the food, and will only begin to search after you have finished. You should vary the hiding places to make sure that the cat has to truly search for the food and doesn't just walk the usual route.

Cats who eat moist food, home-cooked food or raw food don't get their meals in the usual spot, but instead get them partitioned in several daily rations inside small bowls, jam jar lids or something similar, and they are made to search the whole house for their food.

First put a mini portion for your cat in the usual spot. As soon as the cat has finished eating and is looking at you with an indignant expression, show them the second mini portion, walking a few paces with it and then putting it down. Once the cat has eaten this portion too, put the third portion on the top level of the scratching tree. You'll notice that, after some initial scepticism, in a very short time this food search is providing your cat with a lot of fun.

This particular cat in search of treats should not present his owners with any worries about his figure. (Photo: Slawik)

Unwrapping food

The unwrapping of food is an enhanced form of the search. Cats aren't just very dextrous with their paws, they also love to use their paws to shred paper and dig out the object of their desire from somewhere.

You will probably find items in your house that are suitable for testing the unwrapping game with your cat straight away.

Food in a cloth

Take a small redundant hand or tea towel and a few treats. Spread the cloth, place the treats on top and fold up the cloth. Of course you let your cat watch while you're doing this.

The cat will probably try and prevent you from wrapping the treats, but if they wait patiently until you have finished, they will be allowed to unwrap the food straight away.

At the beginning the cat should watch in order to get to know the game. If you just put the food parcel wrapped in the cloth in front of your cat they will not know what to do with it.

Alternatively you can roll up the cloth. At the beginning distribute the treats across the whole length of the cloth, so that the cat gets to be successful straight away after their first attempts to unroll the cloth. The highest level of difficulty is reached when you roll a treat into the first fold of the cloth. The cat will only be able to obtain the treat if they unroll the entire roll right to the end.

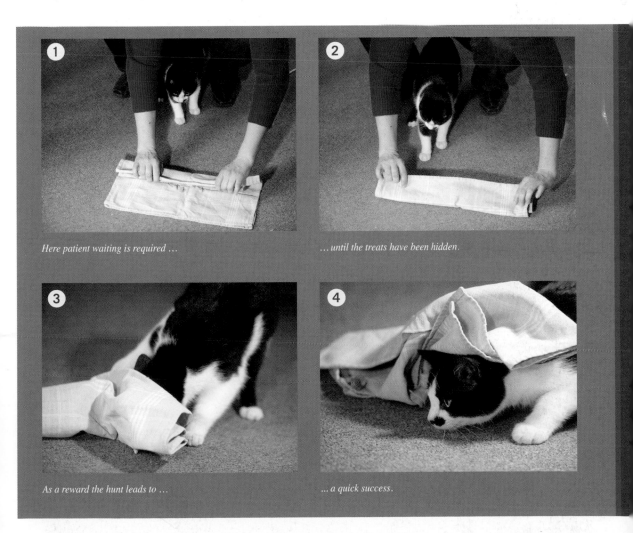

Here patient waiting is required …

…until the treats have been hidden.

As a reward the hunt leads to …

… a quick success.

Indoor cats can occupy themselves very satisfactorily with little food parcels such as these while their owners are working. (Foto: Dbalý)

Unwrapping tea bags

If you have individually wrapped tea bags in the house, you can hide one or two lumps of dried cat food in one of the little paper wrappers. You could also empty the tea bag itself and put the dried food inside.

Stuffed toilet roll

The empty insides of toilet rolls or rolls of kitchen foil can also be stuffed with treats. Close the cardboard tube by putting crunched up newspaper into each end. The cat will roll the rattling and rustling object about investigating it from all sides.

Again, at the beginning the task should be as easy as possible for the cat. Use an ample amount of tasty treats, stuff the newspaper only very loosely into the openings and make sure that the first treats will tumble out straight away as the paper is pulled out. Give your cat some assistance the first few times. Show your cat that they will only reach the treats if they pull out the paper.

As soon as the cat has understood the principle of the game you can increase the difficulty and introduce variations Use several separate shreds of paper to seal the ends – in order for the cat to reach the treats, these will have to be pulled out one by one. To make the cat work harder, stuff the paper more tightly into the ends. Alternate the newspaper and the treats in order to create several treat-containing chambers. Mix dried pasta twirls in with the treats – this creates a nice rattling effect and the cat will increase its efforts.

Who has got the knack?

Cats who have understood the trick with the newspaper will find a new challenge in a closed cardboard tube with holes. Use a pair of nail scissors to cut holes into a cardboard tube, push the ends to the inside so that the tube is relatively tightly sealed, and then add some dried cat food by putting it through the holes.

There you have the perfect pawing toy with a rolling action. The first cardboard tube should have very large holes cut into it, in order to give the cat rapid success. You may have to leave a few treats next to the tube so the cat will start to nudge and push the tube.

Once the cat has got the knack, you can build more difficult food tubes. Make the holes smaller, reduce the number of holes you cut into the tube, put less dried cat food inside, and add other rattling items, such as dried pasta twirls.

For beginners the openings should only be sealed lightly with the paper – you can make the game a bit harder for expert fumblers. (Photo: Slawik)

This tube has been sealed with wooden toy building blocks.
(Photo: Slawik)

Box with mouse holes

Cats love to wait outside holes and nooks and crannies, and they will also stick their paws inside if they can hear a rustling noise or see something interesting. Give your cat a box with mouse holes as a present. For this you need a closed cardboard box. Cut holes into the corners of this box at floor level and, depending on the size of the box, possibly into the sides too. The cat should be able to reach every part of the bottom of the box with their paw. Cut another small hole into the top of the box through which you can throw treats, small balls, furry mice and other things that make a rattling noise, and then the great pawing fun can begin.

Before you start you'll have to explain this game to your cat as well. The best way of doing this is to let the cat watch you while you're preparing the box; this will soon make the cat interested. It's best not to put the first treats through the holes in the top that you made for this purpose. Place the treats near the holes you cut into the corners of the box, so the cat can see them and reach them easily. If the cat has understood that there are good things to be had from these holes, you can roll the treats further inside and eventually drop them inside through the hole in the lid. The cat will probably try to reach the prey through the lid initially, but they will quickly remember that there are other holes that have successfully provided goodies before.

The cardboard box will slide on most surfaces as soon as the cat starts fumbling with it. Some cats don't mind, they just slide after it. Other cats will take advantage of it and push their head against the box quite forcefully to test whether something will rattle within, which will make it worth their while to stick a paw inside. Other cats don't like it at all if the box slides about.

In this case you can stick some anti-sliding material (suitable for your floor) with double-sided sticky tape under the bottom of the box.

The cup and pea game

A cat who has worked out all the aforementioned play ideas without a problem is a suitable candidate for the cup and pea game. For this you need an egg cup, a stable small liqueur glass or a small plastic cup, very tasty treats and a cat who has slept well. Show the cup and treats to the cat and then give them one of the extra tasty treats to give them a taste for it and thus be very motivated. Then you show the cat a further treat, put it on the floor and cover it with the cup.

Which hole offers the best access to the prey?
(Photo: Slawik)

35

The cup game is also good for two players …

…even though, unfortunately, there can only be one winner in the end. (Photos: Slawik)

The cat will be baffled and walk around the cup looking for an opening. Plastic cups fall over easily when a cat nudges them with its nose. Therefore they are just right for beginners at this game. Once the cat has twigged what all this is about, you can move on to heavier cups. A small liqueur glass is quite stable and doesn't fall over so easily. Please don't use thin-walled liqueur glasses. The cat will circle around the cup while purring loudly and push it across the room with their paw until the right momentum is attained. As soon as the cat has developed a taste for this game, you can exchange the very tasty treat for more frugal prey.

To say that the cup game should only be played on a soft surface should be stating the obvious. Glass and stone floors just aren't a good combination.

An even bigger conundrum than knocking over the cup is fishing for treats under a plastic or cardboard plate. With a pair of nail scissors cut a hole of at most one centimetre diameter into the bottom of the plate. Use a serving tray with a raised rim as a surface and place the upturned plastic or cardboard plate on it. Show your cat a treat and then let the treat drop through the hole in the cardboard plate. Hold on to the serving tray. The raised sides of the serving tray prevent the cat from pushing the cardboard plate off as soon as they have got started. If, after several attempts, the cat doesn't manage to turn the plate over, lift the plate and enable your cat to have a hunting success. Hide a further treat in front of the cat's eyes.

In order to keep the game exciting, put a treat under a handkerchief for a change, or offer it to your cat in a half-open matchbox. Hold the matchbox in place during this game. The cat can open the matchbox completely with their paw and capture the prey.

(Photo: animals digital/Brodmann)

Who's scared of water? Games involving water

In contrast to many of their large and small feline cousins in the wild, domestic cats don't tend to be overly enthusiastic about water. However there are exceptions. Many playful kittens find water fascinating and are attracted to it. The Turkish Van cat is a virtual water rat, that's why it is also called the swimming cat.

Even among grown-up members of various other feline breeds you will find the occasional cat who likes to go fishing in puddles, ponds, fountains, watering cans, vases and even toilets. For this kind of housemate there are wonderful games involving water.

A certain amount of dexterity is required. Phoenix is fishing for the treat on the floating plastic flower with his tongue. (Photo: Slawik)

Indoor fountain

Indoor fountains aren't just pretty to look at. They have a beneficial effect on the room climate as well, and the splashing sounds, the movements and the light reflections in the water attract the indoor cat's interest. When adding greenery to your water feature please only use cat friendly non-toxic plants. Your vet, or a knowledgeable flower vendor or gardener, can supply you with the relevant information. In order to keep an element of excitement about the fountain you can put it on a timer. This way it won't run all the time, but only at certain times of day. Because cats love to drink from indoor fountains, make sure the water is of good quality, and clean the fountain regularly. Chemical additives in the water should be avoided.

Fishing permitted

For hobby anglers among cats you can fill a larger container that won't tip over easily with lukewarm water. If you put swimming toys such as plastic lids or balls into this little pond, the cat will attempt carefully to fish the toys out of the water. Some cats can be watched as they push one paw into the water aiming for the toy, then throw it over their shoulder behind them in order to pounce on it and hold it down. For indoor cats who aren't scared of getting their paws wet, you can throw in a toy that will sink slowly to the bottom. Cats tend to find bottle corks posing as fish in the kitty lake extremely fascinating. If there is a feather sticking out of the top of the cork, the cat will happily carry on playing with the prey after capture.

For cats who, in spite of their fascination for the watery element, don't like getting their paws wet, you can offer treats in small floating boats or rafts, which they can retrieve with their mouths.
Small paper boats, small pieces of wood, plastic flowers or empty nutshell halves are all suitable for providing floating transport. If your cat does not have a preferred treat they would be keen to fish for, you can offer a freshly picked blade of kitty grass or a small feather as prey.

Water? Bring it on!

For those cats who aren't averse to water, a dripping or running tap or the jet from a shower head can provide hours of happy entertainment. They sniff the water, accompanied by little sneezes, and touch the water with their paws. Some cats even squeeze their head and body under the running tap while squinting with pleasure. Make sure the water is neither too cold nor too hot.

Bath tub captain

Some cats love to immerse their whole bodies in water, and they really appreciate it if you run them a warm bath every now and then.
Put a low footstool with a bath towel on top into the bath tub. From this vantage point the little cat captain can watch the water run into the bath, and make up their mind at which point they want to dive in. In an only moderately filled bath the cat can go for a paddle to their heart's content, scratch around a bit and fish for submersed or floating toys. Join in the game; this will stimulate the cat's interest even more.

Faramir loves water games – especially if his humans join in.
(Photo: Dbalý)

Make sure that the cat can't slip when entering and leaving the bath. The stool in the bath, together with bath towels placed on the rim of the bath tub and on the floor, offers assistance with getting in and out, as well as providing protection against slipping for human and cat alike – nothing can get in the way of a good splish-splosh now!

Afterwards please ensure that your cat has an opportunity to lick themselves dry in a warm and draught-free spot. Offer the cat a bath towel to snuggle into. If the cat likes it you can help dry off their fur by gently rubbing them dry.

Don't be surprised if your feline bathing enthusiast wants to get in with you next time you're having a bath. However, only allow them to do this if you haven't used any bath additives.

Greetings from the big wide world – extras for indoor cats

As already mentioned at the beginning of the book, smells are of enormous importance to cats. A large part of inter-feline communication happens via smell.

While we humans rely mainly on our eyes in order to register the most important information about changes in our environment, a cat collects impressions of the environment with its nose. Upon entering a room the various smells tell the cat whether everything is in its proper place, who is present, whether they have to refresh their own markings, and whether any strange markings have been left behind by others.

Many indoor cats have not been trained to react in a calm and curious way when confronted by strange things in general, and strange smells in particular. From kittenhood onwards they have lacked experience of a constantly changing environment. In contrast to roaming outdoor cats, they rarely have the opportunity to practise dealing with new things by learning to adapt. Therefore you should offer a good selection of impressions and olfactory experiences to your indoor cat.

Where have you been?

Enable your cat to get a share of the world of smells on the other side of your front door. All the clothes you have been wearing outside smell strange and interesting for your cat.

When you return from a shopping expedition stressed and exhausted, please don't get annoyed if your cat wants to assist you with the unpacking. Take advantage of the opportunity to offer something different to your cat, and put the shopping basket on the floor so they can investigate it.

You can allow the cat to investigate your paper shopping bags and other safe packaging materials, such as plastic trays for fruit or vegetables, muesli cartons, opened envelopes and similar items, for a little while before you throw them away. The handles of carrier bags should be cut off or broken to prevent any risk of the cat getting caught or even strangled in them.

Why not lay out an obstacle course of items brought home from the supermarket for your indoor moggy – no, not food, but a variety of safe packaging materials? Put the shopping basket at the finish. Don't be surprised if the cat doesn't

Outdoor footwear smells very exciting.
(Photo: Slawik)

Full of curiosity: I wonder what was inside this bag?
(Photo: Slawik)

investigate the items in the order you have laid them out. The smells of the various boxes and bags are not all of the same interest to the cat. You would probably go for the most visually attractive looking packaging; the cat on the other hand will home in on those things that smell most interesting. You can also scatter the items you have brought home in various different rooms, or arrange a basket of smells for your cat: Just put all the different items of packaging in the shopping basket, and then let the cat rummage around in it to their heart's content. If you transport your shopping from the supermarket to your home in a cardboard box, you are doing your cat a particular favour: cats love cardboard boxes! They don't just smell exciting, but your cat can also jump into

them, lie down in them, hide inside them and peek over the side. You can turn the cardboard box on its side to create an open cave for your cat. Or you can cut a large hole into one side and turn the box upside down – what a brilliant hiding place for a cat.

Small objects from the natural world

Bring home some pine cones for your indoor cat, or chestnuts, acorns, bits of wood or leaves from a walk in the woods, sea shells from a seaside holiday, or small stones from a holiday in the

Rocks contain lots of smells from nature; therefore they make an exciting item to bring home to your cat.
(Photo: Slawik)

mountains. Your cat will sniff everything with great interest.

It's even more exciting if you hide the items in various rooms, so that the cat can discover something new several times over while doing their rounds of the house. Chestnuts, acorns and sea shells also make very good toys and are, at least for a little while, more interesting than the familiar furry mice or balls. A cardboard box filled with rustling autumn leaves or hay for your cat to dive into in order to retrieve a treat is a well loved variation of the box with rustling newspaper inside – your cat will almost forget about the treats hiding within it. Hay is widely available in rural areas; in towns you can get it from any pet shop, scented with various flavours.

Real trees for indoors

For cat paws that have only ever known carpet and tiles, natural materials are pure luxury. Most cats are very happy to accept climbing and scratching trees made from real tree trunks or thick branches. You can order such trees on the Internet, or build them yourself quite easily. All you need is a little time, an electric drill, woodscrews, wooden boards (available from any builders' merchant at a low price), an anti-sliding mat, possibly corner pieces, rawl plugs and wall screws, and of course a tree trunk or thick branch.

You may be able to find out from a local lumber yard where you can get some waste wood.

The cat garden

Allow your cat to enjoy a real meadow with daisies, yarrow and other herbs and flowers, instead of their usual diet of kitty lawn.

Seed mixtures for a wildflower lawn, herb lawn seeds, or a seed mixture for the greening of roofs are all suitable. Sow the mixture into a flower pot or planter that is not too deep but fairly wide. A bright sunny spot in your house is sufficient in order to bring this piece of nature into the home – you don't even need a balcony.

(Photo: Slawik)

You can train a cat – it's cat's play!

'You can't train a cat'. This is the generally accepted opinion, and if by training you mean obtaining blind obedience, then you'd be quite right. Notwithstanding this, cats are very intelligent animals who possess a lifelong ability to react to changing environmental and life situations, and who keep on learning.

If you as the owner know how cats learn and what motivates them, or rather what inhibits them, you will be able to modify your cat's behaviour by means of training or proper upbringing.

Utterly different – and yet they get on very well with each other.
(Photo: Slawik)

Cats are not dogs

During their long evolutionary history cats have never lived in packs, and therefore do not live as adults in circumstances of dependency. Cats hunt by themselves, and female cats can raise their young by themselves. Adult tomcats don't need anyone in order to survive. Many cats are very social creatures and like living in groups, but they are not dependent on this way of life.

If cats develop associations with others of any species, they do it by choice, and not because they have been programmed genetically to live in a social group. For example, in order to avoid aggressive conflicts in the pack wolves have developed a very complex repertoire of communication, in which appeasement, as well as active and passive submission, play major roles. Cats lack these means of communication.

Of course our domestic dogs are not wolves, but they cannot deny their genetic relationship with the wolf. Dogs have always reacted to punishment and to the unpredictable behaviour of their owners with appeasement behaviours. When threatened by their social partner, the human being, cats on the other hand keep their distance and withdraw. Methods of upbringing that are based on the correction of undesirable behaviour by punishment, or that work with the use of force – methods that are often applied by human beings – are completely counter-productive when it comes to cats.

Of course this statement is not intended to imply that punishment should be used in the upbringing of dogs or any other animal. It's just that dogs – in contrast to cats – don't refuse to cooperate straight away if we do so.

How do cats learn?

Cats learn about success and failure. Worthwhile behaviour is displayed more often; conversely,

A nose to nose session with a favourite human is one of the very worthwhile occupations in the life of a cat. (Photo: Slawik)

behaviour that is not worthwhile is displayed less frequently. In theory this sounds simple – but how can this be controlled in an everyday situation?

Anything that satisfies the cat's needs at this particular point in time is worthwhile, for example eating, sleeping, going to the toilet or scratching. What is also worth a cat's while is the ability to do whatever they fancy, venturing into the garden for instance, chasing after a bird, having a scrap with a feline partner or turning to their human owner for attention. Everything you give to the cat that they enjoy and have fun with at that instant is rewarding. This can be a treat, a smell, or friendly attention. What a cat may regard as a reward can vary a great deal from individual to individual. Cats don't necessarily consider what constitutes a reward in the same terms as we do. The reward has to match the cat and their current needs in order for the cat to experience it as something positive. To a timid cat who doesn't like to be touched, stroking can seem like a punishment. Even human-orientated cats don't always want to be touched; sometimes they'd much rather nudge your head with theirs, or have a little chat with you.

A normally very playful cat who has just returned from a long excursion will appreciate a little bowl of food a lot more than the offer of a play session. Many cats are very fussy eaters. Fortunately at the same time they are usually great gourmets who tend to have strong preferences for particular delicacies. You will probably know your cat's culinary weaknesses. Take advantage of this! Tasty treats make the best rewards, particularly when you intend to shape new behaviours. Please bear in mind that sugary, spicy and greasy treats from the human dinner table are not suited to your cat's dietary needs.

The main ingredient for a successful upbringing consists of keeping your eyes peeled and recognising when your cat does things you like. It is exactly these behaviours that you should reward, and your cat will subsequently display them more frequently.

Behaviours that don't provide the cat with the desired success, or satisfy a need, are not worthwhile. However, behaviours for which there are more worthwhile alternatives are not worth a cat's while either.

Hence it is completely superfluous to interrupt a behaviour that you dislike by using punishment. Just make sure that your cat gets to know about an alternative that is more worthwhile to them.

Playfully modifying behaviour during daily routines

If you ask any cat owner what annoys them about their cat, they will always name the same bad behaviours.

Very often the problem is the cat being in the way or demanding attention at the wrong time. In the following sections you can read about how to modify such behaviour elegantly and playfully.

Bright-eyed and bushy-tailed

Are you one of those pitiable human beings who are worked on by their cats early every morning until they get out of bed?

Do you eventually get up peevishly just to placate the cat? You have trained your cat very well! If your cat keeps nudging your cheek for long enough, carefully inserts a claw into your nostril,

Cats can be really annoying – especially when you want to have a lie-in and dear little kitty wants to get on with her list of joint daily activities. (Photo: Richter)

goes walkies on top of you, miaows or jumps about on the bed, you are sure sooner or later to show a reaction.

You will probably have been advised before that you should absolutely ignore your cat's antics for as long as it takes until the cat has learned that you no longer react at all. The cat will then stop the behaviour in question. This elimination of a behaviour, as it is called in scientific jargon, usually works very well. However, there is usually an initial reaction to the attempts to eliminate a behaviour: this involves a spiteful aggravation of the behaviour. Your little livewire

will show you exactly what this means when you attempt to ignore them in the mornings. The cat will redouble their efforts to get a reaction out of you. They won't miss any trick that has ever proved successful in the past, and they will also think of new ways to get what they want. Your cat will develop stamina and perseverance beyond anything you ever thought possible. Every time you think with relief that things are getting better at last, for the next two days the cat will work even harder. Your cat will in all probability win this war of attrition, because a very wide awake and very motivated cat has a decisive advantage over a tired and worn out human. In contrast to the human, the cat can do something active. The owner is condemned to ignore the behaviour and remain absolutely passive.

Your cat is not out to annoy you on purpose. Cats are active at dawn and dusk, and they don't sleep for six to ten hours once a day, but for a few hours several times a day. The cat is simply awake and well rested, wants attention, and probably wouldn't object to breakfast being served either. The cat will be pleased that you've woken up too, nudging you, knocking their head against yours, and will jump around on top of you or start to miaow if they can't get a reaction. In the beginning you probably used to stroke the cat in a soothing manner, but later you may increasingly have moaned and told them off, which may not have been exactly what they wanted, but at least you had reacted and given them some attention. Being told off is also attention, not as nice as being stroked, but for somebody who is after attention, it's better than nothing. No matter what you do, you're bound to reward the cat's behaviour if you do anything at all.

The solution is simple: until now you have rewarded your cat whenever you have spent time with them or even when you got out of bed. Turn the tables on them. Reward the cat for the kind of behaviour you'd like to see, for example lying down quietly. When the cat starts the usual morning ritual and you're trying to ignore them once again, wait until your cat happens to be quiet for a brief moment.

At just this second you turn the light on, say hello to your cat (in that order), cuddle them, play with them or prepare their breakfast, depending on the behaviour your cat is signalling. You have a choice: to continue to be disturbed every morning or to begin a playful training programme with your cat. This training involves you getting up initially, as soon as the cat displays an acceptable behaviour, i.e. being quiet, in order to be able to reward the cat for it. This increases the chance of the cat displaying this behaviour again. Please keep this up for a few days. Ignore your cat's antics and any efforts to get a reaction from you. This means you have to play dead. Your cat will interpret any sound or movement as a signal to get started. As soon as the cat is quiet for a moment, reward them by giving them attention in the above-mentioned manner.

The cat will learn, first, that being quiet is more worthwhile than miaowing and nudging, and, second, to wait until the light is switched on. The light is the signal that you are now prepared to start the day with your cat. For this reason the order of events is so important: first the light, then the attention. You can also use a different signal instead of the light; you could say 'Good morning', for example, or 'Breakfast'. What is important is that this signal is given just before you start to get active. The aim is that the cat will wait for the signal, and not for the alarm clock, movement or waking up sounds.

Once you have baffled your cat with this modified, and for the cat very satisfactory, morning routine for several days in a row, you can begin to draw out the time until you switch on the light. Don't over-reach yourself as a result of this quick success. Increase the time that elapses very slowly, and initially only by a few seconds. The cat goes quiet; you silently count to two and turn on the light. You have now reached the critical point where you need to develop an instinct for the length of waiting time. If the waiting time is too short there is no learning effect, too long and the cat will probably become active in the end, something you should endeavour to avoid. If it does happen, you know that you have waited too long. In this case you should take a few steps backwards. Unfortunately it is impossible to give universally applicable advice regarding the waiting period. It can vary a lot from one cat to another. You'll be on the safe side if you proceed gradually. It is generally advisable to vary the waiting period. When you're at the stage of several seconds, don't have the cat wait a second longer every day. The cat should not be able to predict exactly how long it will take before the light comes on.

As soon as the cat knows that the light will reliably come on every day, and that afterwards you will give them tender love and care, they will increasingly relax while waiting, and patiently hold out during the ever increasing waiting period. The cat has learned that it is worthwhile.

The kitchen helper

Many cats are keen to help with the cooking. To the great annoyance of the owner, the cat prances back and forth between the ingredients, the crockery and the cooker, gets in the way, steals the food and risks burning their paws.

Not to everybody's taste: the cat on the work surface in the kitchen. (Photo: Richter)

If you keep putting treats for your cat on the windowsill whenever you enter the kitchen together, they will quickly find their favourite spot and stay away from the cooking utensils. (Photo: Richter)

Until now you have locked your cat out of the kitchen while cooking is in progress. But, to be honest, you don't actually want to lock kitty out. What could be nicer than a bit of company while doing the cooking? It's just that the cat ought to display some manners. Why don't you teach them to sit on the windowsill or a stool, and just watch instead of running around?

In order to achieve this you temporarily lock the cat out while you are doing the cooking. Between cooking activities take your cat into the kitchen every so often, show them that you have very tasty treats, and put one on the windowsill. The cat will jump on to the windowsill to retrieve it. Have a friendly chat with your cat, and give them a few

more treats there. Should the cat wander around and walk on the work surfaces, turn away and leave the kitchen. The cat will follow you. Now you return to the kitchen with the cat, put a few treats on the windowsill and praise the cat as soon as they jump up on it. Give them a few more treats and a cuddle.

From now on, whenever you enter the kitchen, make sure you have a few kitty treats on you. Every time the cat jumps up on the windowsill, they get a reward. Pay close attention to whether the cat is about to sit down spontaneously, and don't miss this moment. As soon as kitty's rear end touches down on the windowsill, give the cat a treat. You have one second to do this. This is the only way to ensure that the cat will associate the displayed behaviour with the reward. You have to work very fast.

Give the cat a few more treats while they are sitting down, and throw the last one on the floor to make them jump down again. Not every cat will sit down again straight away; some rub against the window frame, others want to rub their heads against yours, or they might reach with their paws towards you. Be patient: every cat will eventually sit down, and that's when the right moment for the treat has come.

After a few days the windowsill will become a place so interesting that the cat will run ahead of you and sit there waiting for you. The work surfaces have completely lost their attraction. Now you can begin to carry out small tasks in the kitchen while the cat is present. As soon as the cat is sitting on the windowsill, take a glass out of a cupboard, and give the cat a treat, then open and close a drawer, and give your cat a treat. Over the next few days basically busy yourself clattering around the kitchen for a bit, while making sure that the cat on the windowsill doesn't feel left out. Go over to the cat regularly, stroke them and tell them how wonderful they are – not forgetting the treats.

Should the cat get up and start wandering about, please ignore this completely. Conversely, as soon as the cat is back on the windowsill praise them immediately and give them their due. Should the cat go walkabout once more, this is a sure sign that you have made them wait too long. Your cat has learned that they will get a reward when they sit on the windowsill. Should you neglect to honour your part of the deal, your cat will remind you. The period of time that the cat is prepared to wait has to be increased slowly through training. If the cat reliably stays on the windowsill, don't take this

for granted, but reward them occasionally. You are pleased when your boss occasionally indicates to you that he or she appreciates your work. For the next few weeks you will probably be much more motivated at work.

How to reward properly

- At the beginning use good quality treats that your cat particularly likes.
- The reward has to be given immediately, at the exact moment that the cat is doing the right thing. You have only got one second to do this.
- At the beginning there must always be a reward.
- As soon as the cat displays the desired behaviour reliably and without hesitation – in anticipation of the reward – you can cut back on the rewards. It is advisable to modify the quality of the reward first.
- If the cat displays the desired behaviour, even if it doesn't get a super reward every time, you can modify the reward frequency. Now the cat doesn't get a reward every time, but is rewarded according to the luck of the draw.

The training of signals

Cats are able to learn the most astonishing things. They can learn to get up on their hind legs, to jump through hoops, to roll over, to lie down in the Sphinx position and many more tricks. Critics find the idea of training independent animals such as cats despicable; they forget, however, that cats will

If there's fun to be had, and the signals are clear, cats can be taught impressive tricks.
(Photo: Slawik)

only cooperate if they are having fun and enjoying doing it. You can't force a cat to do anything they don't want to do, and if you try to coerce a cat, the only result will be complete withdrawal on the part of the cat.

A trusting relationship with the human, free of fear, is the foundation without which any learning with their human is impossible. Two completely mundane behaviours demonstrate how well cats are able to learn in conjunction with their humans.

1. Every human-orientated hungry cat will come running upon hearing the sound of tins of cat food being opened. This means that cats can associate two events with each other.

2. Every human-orientated cat learns, by itself, how to manipulate their human and how to make

the human get out of bed, to play with the cat or prepare food for it. This means that cats learn which consequences are caused by which behaviour, and positive consequences are incredibly motivating to them.

Just like us, cats constantly learn new things. Why leave to chance what kind of lesson your cat is learning at any given moment? If the above-mentioned points are applied sensibly, in cooperation with their human a cat is able to learn anything that their physical and mental abilities permit. A cat will never win the Nobel Prize for chemistry or learn how to drive. However, in a playful manner your cat will learn many things that will make your lives together easier – and tricks as well, if both of you derive pleasure from it.

In order to establish a calling signal, after the chosen word has been uttered the cat gets a treat straight away. (Photo: Slawik)

Come

If your cat comes to you when you call them this is not just good for impressing family and friends – in certain situations it can also be very helpful. It is very easy to teach the cat the relevant calling signal. For this you need tasty treats, a cat who likes hunting treats, a signal word, as well as, repeatedly and spread over a whole day, a few minutes of your time. It's not a good idea to use the cat's name as the signal word, because the cat will normally hear its name in all sorts of other situations, when they are not actually supposed to come. Choose a word signal that does not occur in the cat's everyday life too often, and one that you will be able to remember easily. 'Come to me' or 'come' could be used as calling signals. If, to your ears, this sounds too much like a command, maybe you'd prefer 'cat party'?

If your cat is awake, interested and hungry or, alternatively, in a playful mood, you can start the first training session. Choose a moment when your cat is lying down next to you on the sofa, and is paying attention to you; say your chosen calling signal, then you give the cat a treat without delay. The cat eats it in an instant. Then do the same again: give the signal immediately followed by a treat. At the beginning a few repetitions will suffice. 'This won't make the cat come to me', you

In order to reward the cat for coming to you the treat can be replaced by a favourite toy.
(Photo: Slawik)

will say to yourself, 'he is already here.' True, they won't come to you. Not yet, anyway.

For the next training session you refresh this association while your cat is in close proximity to you. Make sure you give the treat straight after the verbal signal. As soon as you notice that the cat is looking for the treat or licking their chops after you've given your signal, you have reached the next level of training.

Move one step away – the cat will follow. Say your signal and drop the treat on the floor. While the cat is eating it you move a step further away. The moment the cat begins to move in order to follow you, say your signal once more, and drop a treat as soon as the cat has caught up with you. Five or six repetitions are enough. Learning is supposed to be fun and not boring. At the final repetition allow your cat to have a particularly nice treat so that they will have good memories of this final exercise.

The next day repeat once or twice what you have practised up to now, and then embark on working at a slightly greater distance. Please only give the signal when you're quite sure that the cat will come to you. If a noise is distracting the cat, wait until you have their full attention. Feel your way forward step by step until the moment has come when you walk through the door, around the corner and call your cat from there. If you have done your preparations well, the cat should be with you straight away.

During every training session the environment is part of the learning process. This means that things the cat can do to perfection in the living room can't automatically be done in the bedroom or garden as well. Therefore you have to practise in various different quiet locations. Once that works well, you can do the exercise even with

increasing distractions going on at the same time.

Try to resist the temptation to achieve everything in one day. Two to four training sessions with four to six repetitions per day are plenty. Within a few days, the cat (if they are awake) will indeed come running to you when called, in anticipation of a treat, even from another room. However, you'll need a little more practice for the cat to come to you reliably from the garden as well.

If your cat has a favourite toy for which they will drop everything else you can of course use this toy instead of food. It should be a toy that is played with by the cat on the spot, not one that you need to throw. From now on you should only use this particular toy when you have called the cat to you.

The place mat

You're probably familiar with this situation: you have an appointment, you're late, gathering together keys, mobile phone, handbag, and then you suddenly discover a stain on your trousers that will quickly need to be changed – and every step you take your cat nearly trips you up. Or you have a visitor who is not best pleased to have a cat climb all over them spreading cat hairs.

As much as we enjoy our cats communicating with us and demanding our attention, there are moments when this behaviour can be very disruptive. If only they would sit in a particular place. Why 'if only'? Tell the cat, and they will – on the condition that you have practised with them beforehand.

A suitable signal that you can use to tell your cat to remain in a certain spot can be a small cloth, a small blanket or a newspaper.

Teach the cat to go and sit on the cloth as soon as they see it. Many cats display a clear preference for certain materials; this makes choosing a place a lot easier. Tomcat Max is magically attracted by newspaper. Patting a page of newspaper will suffice to ask him to lie down on top of it immediately. If your cat doesn't seem to have any obvious preference, choose a material which you believe to be pleasant to lie on for your cat.

Show your cat this little blanket, about the size of a guest towel, when they are awake, interested, and not in a mood for boisterous play. It can't do any harm to make a bit of a fuss or a show when spreading out the cloth. Without attracting attention you can also put a few treats on top of it. Your cat will come running full of curiosity to see if there's anything interesting going on. They will eat the treat, sniff the cloth, and probably leave again. Let them. Put some new treats on the cloth and make some interesting noises. The cat will come to check it out, and wow, there are some more treats on the blanket, again and again in quick succession. Finally you throw a treat in order to make the cat walk away from the blanket, pack it up and tidy it away. Practise this with your cat for one or two days in small play sessions. Now your cat should come running as soon as you spread out the blanket. As soon as the cat walks straight towards the blanket to check for treats stop putting the treats on it beforehand. To make up for it reward your cat amply (you've not forgotten about the one second, have you?) as soon as they put even just a single paw on the blanket. Be generous. At the beginning the cat doesn't have to stand on the blanket with all four paws. The cat has already recognised after the first few exercises that there is a connection between the blanket and the treats. Now they will learn that they can make the treats appear by stepping on the blanket. Have the cat test this four or five times;

this is enough for the time being. This exercise may look simple, but it requires a lot of concentration on the part of the cat, and you as well, because you are trying hard to stick to the one second reward window. Please bear in mind that any exaggerated expectations take away the joy of learning and trying things out.

As soon as your cat sits down, or even settles on the blanket, praise them in a way that they'll appreciate, stroke them and give them a treat. Your attentions towards the cat should not be the kind that would be likely to get them overexcited. You

Faramir has learned to step on the white cloth …

don't want your cat to work up a mood for play, but to lie there happy and relaxed. You must be the one who ends the exercise. Before the cat gets up of their own accord and walks off the blanket, throw them a treat. As soon as the cat is on their way to get it, fold up the blanket, tidy it away, and carry on with your daily chores.

At this point during the training it is important that the moment you tidy away the blanket you go back to your daily routines, and put an end to the cat's pampering programme. This way the cat will quickly learn the connection between the blanket and being spoilt. As a consequence the blanket will become an irresistible spot for the cat, which they will associate with joy, relaxation and attention. After many repetitions the blanket alone will trigger all the positive feelings that the cat had been having whilst on the blanket before with treats. At some point you can substantially reduce the attention, treats and stroking (but please never stop them completely) and also practise in different locations. You don't need a word signal for this exercise. The blanket itself is the signal.

...and to lie down on it.
(Photos: Slawik)

(Photo: Slawik)

An obstacle course across the house

Why not build a proper fitness trail right across the house? Simple obstacles that cater to the cat's particular preferences offer a lot of fun for cat and human.

Use your imagination when building the obstacles, as long as you take your cat's physical abilities into account and ensure that the cat is not scared of the obstacles. If you begin with separate, easy to overcome obstacles, even older cats can be encouraged to play these games; it will work wonders for their health and agility.

What do you need as props?

There are barefoot parks for humans where they can experience how it feels to walk on different materials. For cosy indoor moggies you could put down a few soft pillows, or a big flowerpot tray or baking tray filled with round pebbles.

For a cat who enjoys physical movement you can use a stool and several tins for a slalom, and fashion a tunnel from a shopping bag with the handles and bottom cut off. You can also clamp a wide board between two chairs to make a bridge.

You can also involve friends or family members to form part of the fitness trail. Outstretched arms and legs make great hurdles. Children standing on all fours can become living bridges. Unflappable cats can climb or jump over small children who are crunched up into little parcels, or they can walk around them.

In order to familiarise the cat with this game and to show them how much fun they could have by joining in, you should pay attention to the behaviours the cat displays frequently in everyday situations. You should take these preferences into account when designing the obstacles.

For a cat who likes to jump you can build the kind of stations that require them to jump high or over long distances. A suitable obstacle for a more laid-back cat would only require them to walk across or around it. For a water lover you can build a water-filled ditch to wade across. A box filled with rustling paper is just right for a young daredevil to dive into.

The props you need for a fitness trail – with the cat as the main protagonist.
(Photo: Dbalý)

The target stick for guiding

It would be simple to hold a much desired toy or treat in front of the cat's nose and to lure them across the obstacles with it. Unfortunately some cats are so greedy that they are impossible to guide in this way. Young cats in particular can fall if they don't pay attention while dangling after the treat. It is difficult or impossible to play this game with a cat who is overexcited. Therefore it is worthwhile to have the cat practise beforehand, in small steps, how to calmly follow a target stick.

Choose a longish stick, one end of which you mark with a different colour of paint. This way you can see the tip while you're guiding the cat with the target stick. An old radio aerial is ideal, because you can adjust its length. Before you can deploy the target stick, the cat needs to be conditioned to the sound of a clicker or another suitable sound.

The trick with the click

The importance of having the reward follow within one second in order to allow the cat to make the association between a behaviour and the reward is often mentioned. Clicker training can help us to react very quickly and makes it much easier for the cat to learn as well.

In order to be able to use the clicker you first associate the click sound with giving the treat within one second. This requires a lot of concentration, but is surprisingly successful: after repeating this enough times – this may vary between cats – the click triggers the same feelings and physical reactions as a treat does. This association will only last enduringly if the promise of a treat is kept as often as possible. This means that the click almost invariably has to be followed by an actual treat.

Fortunately, after successful conditioning, you have more time for this than half a second.

Using the clicker you can achieve very specific successes, because the method allows you to let the clicker-conditioned animal know the exact point at which they have done something right. A marker such as a clicker is particularly helpful for exercises that require a movement to be executed in a specific way. How else are you supposed to reward the cat right at the moment when they are about to learn to jump to a particular height, for instance?

However, as described earlier in this book, the clicker can also be used very well in everyday situations.

If you are interested in clicker training, we can recommend a good book on the subject (see page 107).

With the clicker Faramir is learning to follow the target stick calmly.
(Photo: Slawik)

We then proceed as follows: wait until your cat is in the mood to play, then call them. Coming from the side (never directly from the front) with a calm hand, hold the target stick close to the cat's nose and wait. The moment the cat, full of curiosity, goes up to the stick with their nose, you click once, give the cat a treat, and move the target stick out of the cat's field of vision behind your back. Once the cat has eaten the treat, with a slow movement you move the stick towards the cat from the other side, clicking once more as soon as the cat touches the stick with their nose then giving them a treat. After repeating this four or five times you should stop.

For the following training sessions you can hold the tip of the stick a little further away from the cat's nose, so the cat has to take a step towards it in order to touch it. Only make a click when the nose is touching the marked tip – not if the cat bites into it or puts their paws on it.

Short training sessions firm up the behaviour. To avoid being tempted into overdoing it, you can limit the number of treats you put to one side for this to four or five. Once the cat has got all the treats, this automatically concludes the exercise. Repeat this game during several exercise sessions, and hold the target stick at nose level in such a way that the cat will run towards it in order to touch it. Now practise holding the tip a short distance below or above nose level. Please remember to move in a very placid manner, because you don't want the cat to play with the stick.

As soon as this works well, move on to the next stage. The target stick is held at nose level. When the cat approaches it, withdraw it with a calm movement in the same direction in which the cat is moving, so that the cat follows the tip of the stick. Practise this at a short distance at first, before you increase the level of difficulty.

Hold the target stick still once more. As soon as the cat touches it with their nose, make a click and give the cat a treat. Practise following the target stick in short exercise sessions. Finally, when you hold the stick still, the click and the treat are given. Try taking different routes. Be happy with your cat if the exercise is a success. Once the cat follows the target stick you can begin to guide them around an easy obstacle such as a stool. When that's done successfully, stay there and make a click as soon as the cat touches the tip of the target stick with their nose. Remove the target stick from the cat's field of vision and give them a treat.

The cat has now learned to follow the target stick around an obstacle. So far you have built a suitable course with very few obstacles. If your cat is awake and in a mood to play, you can start! Remember to have the treats handy, and call the cat. Begin the game with an announcement, for example 'Go!', or whatever you prefer – what matters is that you say the same thing every time. The cat quickly learns that this marks the start of the game. Guide your cat over the first obstacle at a speed that enables them to keep up with the tip of the target stick. Reward the cat as soon as they have overcome one of the obstacles, and make it obvious how pleased you are. Once the cat has worked up enough motivation, you can tackle another obstacle.

Should the cat refuse an obstacle, try to think what could be the reason. Perhaps the cat doesn't want to climb over the stool? In this case, guide them around the stool. Reward them, and call it a day. It is important to end the game with a positive experience for the cat, in order to make sure that they will keep enjoying it. To end the game, always use the same word, and tidy the props away afterwards.

The obstacle course with kids and cat

Cats who are used to a bit of rough and tumble can play on the obstacle course with children as well, if the children have been shown how to do it by grown-ups and the cat is able to follow the target stick reliably. A game with lively cats and younger children can be quite boisterous. For the cat it can be de-motivating if a child tries to push them across an obstacle when things don't seem to be moving quickly enough.

Just organise a little competition among the children. Whoever manages to guide the cat across an obstacle with the help of the target stick, without touching the cat, will be allowed ceremoniously to present the cat with its favourite treat afterwards. This is also a useful tool to counteract increased noise levels when a game may get a bit hectic. One child concentrates on guiding the cat while the other children watch with beady eyes to ensure that the cat is really not being touched.

Don't let children play this game with the cat unsupervised. Children have to learn to end the game while the cat is still motivated. If the cat suddenly doesn't want to play any longer and walks away, sweets can serve as a reward provided the child lets the cat get away without bothering it.

With adult instruction and supervision children can do a good job of guiding a cat across various obstacles with a target stick. (Photo: Dbalý)

(Photo: Slawik)

Acrobatics for cats

'Look what I can do!' is what many a cat would proudly say to their human after successfully performing an acrobatic trick. Learning simple tricks is fun for human and cat alike, and it also promotes mental and physical abilities. By working out these tricks together, human and cat get to know each other better and intensify their relationship.

The best way is to recognise which behaviours are displayed frequently by the cat, and to promote these talents during training. Tricks are nothing more than displaying a particular behaviour following a given signal. With skill, timing and a sensitive approach, together you can even achieve spectacular tricks such as exercises on top of a ball.

Dancing

A cat turning on his own axis is nothing unusual. If your cat turns round reliably as soon as the human gives the signal, this is already a small trick – albeit one fashioned from natural behaviour.

Useful signals are visual signals, such as finger and hand movements, audible signals and props. Cats are particularly aware of movements, and will easily learn visual signals.

Capturing

A natural and fully displayed behaviour is 'captured' if it is followed – within one second – by a click and a treat.

In order to introduce a certain behaviour, the cat has to learn two things. On one hand the cat needs to know what they should do when the signal is given; on the other hand the cat needs a good reason why they should do it. Cats are not very good at following orders, and they won't do anything that isn't worth their while. Therefore, before you introduce a signal, you should persuade your cat to enjoy the desired behaviour so much that they will carry it out voluntarily and frequently.

Some cats will revolve around their own axis as a way of greeting their human. Others display this behaviour while impatiently waiting for their food bowl. Choose the location in which your cat offers the 'dance' spontaneously and start the training immediately. If you're quick enough, you can give the cat an extra tasty treat every time they have turned around their axis. Once again, remember: you have at most one second.

It's even easier if the cat has been conditioned to work with the clicker. To the cat the click always represents an end to the displayed behaviour. Quickly throw them a treat in order to make them come to you to fetch it. After the reward wait until the cat does another about turn, and reward them once more; don't coax or lure the cat into displaying the desired behaviour. The cat is supposed to offer it of their own accord, and to follow the exercise mentally as well. After repeating this over a period of a few days, the cat will begin to do about turns in the location of the exercise, in order to receive the next treat.

The time must be right for introduction of the signal. At the beginning the signal has no meaning for the cat. Therefore it doesn't make a lot of sense to give a signal when the cat is on their way towards the exercise location. Wait for the moment when you can be sure that the cat will display the desired behaviour – and just at that moment, when the cat is looking at you and is about to turn around, show them a movement, such as describing circles with an outstretched finger. Make sure you stand perfectly still while doing this, and show the cat the signal with a clear movement.

As soon as the cat has done an about turn, reward them as usual. If the cat starts to turn around again, make the signal and give the treat. Repeat this several times as well. After you have introduced a finger or hand signal your cat will pay more attention to your hands.

If the cat does about turns without your signal, this is fine and will still be rewarded at this stage. At the next stage you only reward the cat for about turns that have been done in connection with the

Some cats greet their human by performing a 'dance' – it's only a small step to doing this when prompted by a signal. (Photo: Dbalý)

signal. Now the cat is learning to distinguish between dancing and about turns without a signal. The only about turns that are worthwhile now are those that follow your signal.

Help your cat to learn this distinction. Show the signal clearly while your cat is looking towards you, and as soon as the cat prepares to turn. From this point onwards only reward the cat when they perform a turn following your clearly displayed signal. Your signal takes on a meaning, because the cat receives information before the dance about whether to expect a reward. It is important that you really do give the cat a treat every time they carry out the behaviour properly following your signal. It is only natural that the cat will increasingly wait for your signal, because who likes to make an effort for no reward?

Walking through the legs

Tricks, of course, consist of a sequence of movements that the cat is not going to offer as a finished product, which makes it difficult to control them by signal only. Cats who will do a slalom or jump through hoops of their own accord are comparatively rare.

If you want to teach tricks like that to your cat, you have to teach them the complex sequence of movements first. Once this has been achieved, you can assign a signal to it. In order to teach the movement it is best to start backwards, and to split the trick mentally into its separate components. These are put together again in small steps in conjunction with the cat. This is called 'shaping'.

Shaping
During shaping the desired end behaviour is split into a series of smaller preliminary stages. After the first reinforced preliminary behaviour with the potential of becoming a trick – this could just be a look or a small head movement – any modification of this behaviour in the direction of the final desired behaviour is reinforced.

In order to walk through your legs, the cat should be on your left side to begin with. When you advance one step with your right leg, the cat is supposed to walk through your legs to the other side, next to the right leg. At the end you put your left leg next to your right leg, closing the gap.

Make sure that you are not going to be disturbed for the next few minutes. Take the clicker in your left hand and about six treats in your right hand.

Call your cat. Say 'go!' (or another start word, always use the same one for this trick) and give the cat a treat about ten centimetres away on the outside of your left foot. As soon as the cat has eaten it and takes a look to see what else you may have for them, take a step forward with your right foot. The cat will probably notice the movement and look in that direction. Observe your cat, stay calmly rooted to the spot and wait. Make a click the moment the cat is looking through the gap between your legs.

Give the cat a treat so that the cat's head is pointing in the direction in which they are supposed to move. As soon as the cat casts another look through your legs, give them a click and a treat. Should the cat run around after the click (a click always means breaking off the behaviour) start the exercise afresh. To start with give your cat a treat ten centimetres away from the side of your left foot. Don't talk and please don't lure the cat. The cat is supposed to work out through trial and error which behaviour leads to success. This can only be done if the cat is allowed to make mistakes. This game provides a mental challenge for your cat. Practise it in short exercise sessions, during which you feed the cat about five to six treats, then have a break.

The starting place should always be next to your left leg. Take the step forwards with your right leg. During several exercise sessions on different days, reinforce any look your cat may take through your legs with a click and a treat.

If the cat is looking through your legs purposefully and frequently, omit the click and wait. The baffled cat will perhaps try to take a step – and this is rewarded immediately by a click and a treat. Put down the treat in such a way as to point the cat in the right direction. If your cat is

This is how the slalom is practised. As soon as Faramir takes a look through the human's legs, he gets a click and a treat.

The next treat is pointing the cat in the right direction.

sitting down a lot during this exercise, put down the treat in a spot that requires them to get up in order to retrieve it. This increases the probability that your cat may get up, should the click fail to materialise. Please don't lure the cat, just be patient.

During further exercise sessions you can point the cat in the right direction – until they have walked through your legs. Make a click and put down the treat ten centimetres away from the side of the right leg once the cat has done a complete walk through your legs. Your cat has displayed the desired behaviour to completion for the first time. Do show your cat how pleased you are. After taking a break, repeat this exercise.

To prevent your cat from tearing constantly through your legs all the time, begin this exercise always in the same way. Turn it into a small ritual: call the cat, say 'go' or your chosen start word – you must always use the same one – and give your cat a treat on your left side (without a click). Once this has been eaten, and the cat is looking towards you, immediately put the right foot forward. The cat is now walking through your legs; make a click and give the cat a treat next to your right leg. Then let your left foot catch up and say a final word to your cat, such as 'done'.

When practising tricks it is generally useful to let your cat know when you are about to begin the exercise and when you are about to end it; in this way the cat learns to distinguish between everyday situations and exercise situations.

Faramir has walked through the legs for the first time, and receives a treat next to the right leg as a reward. (Photos: Dbalý)

fences or narrow walls. Other training equipment such as tables, sideboards and shelves is forbidden territory for many cats.

Games that involve balancing are ideal for honing skills such as sure-footedness, the ability to concentrate and a sense of balance. These games are important for indoor cats in order to preserve their poise. In addition these games are a lot of fun.

Many large modern scratching trees are designed to have ropes or boards covered in carpet, fabric or sisal running between the trunks. Others are made from real tree parts with branches. On scratching trees like this even an indoor cat can learn new skills negotiating narrow bridges. Wall-mounted shelves offer excellent balancing opportunities for our indoor moggies.

From high up, cats are also able to have a great panoramic view and access to an additional level of the room.

Balancing act

Cats are famous for their elegant and easy sense of balance. Thanks to their physique and their long tails they are optimally equipped for doing masterful tightrope walks.

However, even cats need to practise to reach perfection, and if they don't, they lose any superior ability over time. The importance of regular training is obvious when you observe kittens at play. As soon as they get distracted and lose their concentration they'll even fall off wide benches, chairs or boxes.

In nature there are plentiful opportunities for cats to practise their balancing skills. Inside houses there are no trees with thin branches,

Caution: cats with kittens

Cat mothers with their kittens should not have access to rooms equipped with shelving. Many a cat mother will find a new nest in a protected place high up under the ceiling. She will do many kinds of acrobatic stunts in order to transport her kittens there in her mouth. Accidents do happen, and a kitten may fall to the ground.

Balancing facilities are a real asset for every house with feline residents, but many an elderly cat who has spent their life in an environment lacking such facilities has to re-learn the ability to walk on narrow or rounded gangways, albeit a bit closer to the ground.

If they have sufficient training opportunities cats are uniquely sure-footed balancing artists.
(Photo: Brodmann)

Building balancing facilities

To begin with you should build a balancing facility that is not too high. You can clamp a board that is fifteen to twenty centimetres wide between two chairs.

The board must not bend or break under the cat's weight. The distance between the chairs should be approximately twice as long as the cat's body. For a small female Burmese this distance will be shorter than for a large Maine Coon tom.

Some cats will be tempted just to jump across by the wide seat area of the chair on the other side of the board. Use chairs or stools that have a small uninviting seat area, or use a board that has the same width as the chair's seat area.

Balancing exercises

There are three ways you can encourage a cat to balance:

- Have the cat follow a trail of treats.
- Guide the cat across with a target stick.
- Teach the cat to start balancing when prompted by a signal.

Follow the treat

The first method is to lure the cat with treats. If your cat is in a playful mood, call them on to a chair and give them a treat. Put the treats on to the board at intervals of ten centimetres.

The cat concentrates on the treats and will run from treat to treat across the board and stop every so often in order to eat the treats. The balancing act isn't our main concern when using this method, but the collecting and eating of the treats.

This way of doing things will become problematical if you modify the level of difficulty of your balancing facility. Some cats become very hectic with this method. The treats can fall off a narrow board very easily, and the cat will jump after the treat instead of concentrating on the balancing act.

You can place treats along a fairly wide board. (Photos: Dbalý)

Once a cat is familiar with the target stick, it is possible to guide them purposefully and calmly. (Photo: Dbalý)

Guiding with target stick and clicker

The second possibility is to use a target stick in conjunction with a clicker. When the cat has learned to follow the target stick, they can be guided calmly across the board. When the cat has reached the other side, stay put with the target stick. Make a click when the cat touches the tip with their nose and then give a treat. The cat gets the treat only after the balancing act.

Balancing by trial and error

With the help of the clicker you can practise the balancing act like a small trick, which the cat learns through trial and error. The cat is neither being lured nor led. Cats benefit from being required to use their minds and to concentrate, and are able to take the initiative.

You have conditioned your cat to react to the clicker and they have learnt to follow the target stick. Make sure you're not going to be disturbed during the next few minutes. Keep some small treats and the clicker at hand. Sit down next to the board between the chairs and guide your cat to the chair with the target stick. Make a click when the cat is on the chair, give them a treat and put the target stick to one side.

The balancing board is new to the cat and they will look at it or sniff it. Make a click immediately and give your cat a treat. For every move the cat makes towards the board make a click.

If the cat sits down on the chair, make a click as soon as they as much as look at the board. Place the treat that you're holding in your hand in front of the cat's paws. Repeat the exercise, giving clicks for a head movement in the direction of the board four or five times, then end the session and have a break.

In the next exercise session, when the cat looks purposefully towards the board, do not click when the cat just looks once. The cat will be confused because the action isn't followed by a click, and may get up in order to look more obviously towards the board. Affirm the action of getting up with a click. If the cat stays sitting down, click for looking towards the board as before, and give the cat the treat in a way that forces them to get up and take a step towards the board. Conclude the exercise session with this.

Make sure that you repeat this exercise always using the same chair as a starting point. In the following exercise sessions make a click when the cat puts one paw on the board, then two paws,

three paws, four paws ... and bingo, the cat has walked across the short board. Make a click, give your cat a particularly tasty treat, and conclude the exercise with this success.

For advanced and expert balancers

Once your cat can walk across this first simple obstacle you can increase the balancing distance in increments of about twenty centimetres. When a longer distance poses no problem to your cat either, and they walk across it with confident steps, you can choose a narrower balancing board. Once again, start with a short distance. The narrower the board you choose, the more your cat will concentrate on not falling off. Allow the cat to walk across without praising or pushing them. For cats who are enthusiastic balancers you can increase the level of difficulty further by

Faramir has understood what this exercise is all about – he gets up and starts walking. (Photo: Dbalý)

modifying the surface of the balancing course or replacing the narrow board with a broomstick.

Every time you modify the width and structure of the balancing course you should start once more with a short distance of about twice the length of the cat. It is very helpful for the cat to be able to focus on a certain point on the other side, particularly during a difficult balancing act – therefore don't obscure the cat's view ahead.

How to get a couch potato moving

Old, sick, injured and other cats who don't like to move or are not allowed to move, because they are restricted to a cage or have a plaster cast for example, can be mentally stimulated with a very simple game. The cat will also carry out small physical movements. For cats who feel inhibited in the presence of human beings and don't move a lot as a result, this can be a great game for removing their inhibitions.

Even for rather lazy cats who don't like to move much there are little games that will get them going! (Photo: Richter)

Every movement – in this case lowering the head – can be rewarded with the clicker,
and you can specifically prompt various behaviours.
(Photos: Dbalý)

During this game the cat is rewarded for small physical actions and encouraged to display them more clearly, and above all more frequently. For this all you need is an awake cat, some favourite treats and a marker such as a clicker. For cats who move very little it makes sense to give them part of their food ration in this way.

It doesn't matter whether the cat is standing up, sitting down or lying down. Sit down close enough to the cat that you can hand them treats comfortably with your outstretched arm. It's best to sit slightly sideways on to the cat, and avoid staring into their face, especially the eyes. Among cats, fixing them with a gaze and staring at them are not considered expressions of politeness. When the cat makes a movement – even the tiniest movement – react immediately, mark the behaviour with a click and give the cat a treat. You can, for example, reinforce movements of the ears, head or paws. In addition you can choose movements such as opening the mouth, yawning or squinting.

The cat can offer further movements such as lifting the paws, stretching or walking (including backwards) while sitting down or standing up. You should not give clicks for behaviours that you might later find undesirable should the cat start to display them more frequently.

Cats understand surprisingly quickly what this game is about. The offer of being spoiled by their human with edible treats and entertainment makes even the most committed couch potato happy to join in. You too will probably be very pleased when you see how the cat is reacting and getting involved in the game. As soon as the cat is familiar with this game, they will repeat their favourite moves more frequently.

These initially very small movements, and sometimes merely the beginnings thereof, can now be worked on to make them more pronounced, by reinforcing only the desirable ones. This way the cat learns to carry out movements more frequently, more clearly and with more purpose.

As each movement is no longer followed by a click and a treat, the game has become more exciting for the cat. Instead of awarding clicks for the same movement pattern every time, at the beginning try to capture various different movements in several playing sessions. It may not seem like it, but this game is very tiring for the cat. Take ten to fifteen treats and finish the game when these have been eaten. Have a longish break before starting on another round of play, because you don't want to overtax the more placid cat, or one that is ill or injured.

(Photo: Slawik)

For strategists –
the fumbling board for cats

To search, discover and capture – there is nothing more exciting for a cat. Action is created by motivation, and for this, fumbling boards offer suitable situations in many different variations. Playing with the fumbling board means being physically and mentally active; cats can exercise their skills and have lots of fun at the same time.

Hidden inside the playing stations are treats or sought-after toys, which can be captured using the appropriate strategy. The cat has to think, decide, try things out and gather experience in order to be successful. Cats can work at their own speed and busy themselves with the fumbling board for as long as they like – whether their human is present or not.

The fumbling board, with fumbling modules, rummaging modules and tongue modules.
(Photo: Slawik)

What is a fumbling board for cats?

A fumbling board for cats consists of a non-slip base on to which various fixed or movable playing units, or modules, have been mounted. Treats or toys are hidden inside these modules for capture by the cat. The modules are available in three basic versions:

- 🐾 Fumbling modules (fixed or flexible) are filled with treats or toys that cats can capture using their paws.
- 🐾 Rummaging modules (or fumbling boxes) are containers that are filled with inedible materials. The cat digs around for treats or toys that have been scattered among the materials, thereby using their entire body.
- 🐾 Tongue modules (fixed or flexible) are playing units with small compartments from which the cat can capture food in liquid or solid form by using their tongue. Tongue modules are not suitable for offering toys.

The cat's tongue

The long, rough cat's tongue is very agile and a useful tool. Its surface is covered with papillae and rasp-like projections or barbs that face backwards, which are helpful for the transport of prey, grooming and drinking. For drinking the tongue is used as a ladle.

The modules can be made from various different materials. Almost anything that doesn't allow cats to extract the food with their mouths unimpeded is suitable for this. If you leave a fumbling board in place for long-term use it is very important that no materials that are dangerous to cats have been used. Loose bits of string, materials that may splinter, pointy edges, and loose parts that can be swallowed, are not suitable. In addition the entire playing station should be easy to clean, or be replaced on a regular basis.

Many of the play ideas presented in this book can be mounted as playing modules, in a slightly modified form, on a fumbling board for cats.

Fixed modules

Fixed modules are immovable structures that are mounted as playing modules on the base. In order to make a tenon module, drill several holes (one centimetre deep) into the base with about two to three centimetres between them. Stick the tenons, which are at least four centimetres long, into these holes and stick them down with wood glue if necessary.

Porous materials and those with a large surface area will adhere particularly well if they have been stuck down with glue or a hot glue gun. Modules such as a piece of bamboo, the lids of spray cans, yoghurt tubs or bottles should additionally be screwed down; always use washers underneath the screw heads. If very flexible material such as plastic is fixed only with glue, it will tear off easily under the impact of a cat's paws.

Tenon modules are exciting and are easy to make. In this case bottle corks have been glued to a base. (Photo: Slawik)

See-through materials – a special challenge

Cats have to learn how to deal with modules made from see-through materials. Although they have excellent night vision and only need about a sixth of the amount of light we do, they can't see details as clearly at a short distance as a human being. In order to investigate objects in close proximity to the mouth, they make use of their very sensitive whiskers. They react very well to moving objects while stationary prey is difficult to locate for a cat. For locating treats in a see-through container whiskers are of no use.

Therefore it is not surprising that these reputedly brilliant hunters often end up hopelessly fumbling around. However, after a few days and with a lot of practice they will have learned to hit the opening straight away.

A fumbling ball cut from the bottom part of a plastic bottle with a bulge is a suitable see-through module. The diameter of the opening should be small enough to make it impossible for the cat to stick their head inside the module. For added safety you should make a small air hole in the ball. The edges where the ball has been cut must be smoothed with sandpaper.

In order to make a fumbling tunnel, cut off the neck of a tall plastic bottle diagonally. Cut an oval-shaped hole of about three to four centimetres into the side and near the bottom of the bottle. This bottle will be screwed to the base lying on its side.

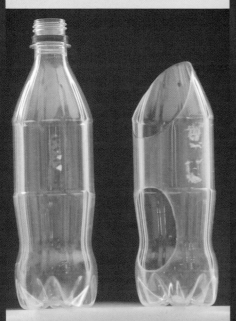

This is how to make a stable, see-through fumbling tunnel from a bottle …

…which is very popular with the cats. (Photos: Slawik)

Movable modules

Flexible modules are structures that can be moved or that contain movable parts, and which are mounted on the base board as playing units.

Flexible elements include, for example, plastic or cardboard tubes that can be twiddled, drawers made from matchboxes, or bottles.

A challenge for expert fumbling board fumblers is a bottle with a treat sitting on a false bottom that can be pulled out. (Photo: Slawik)

Modules like these are suitable for intrepid masters of the pawing technique.

Materials used for the twiddling bottle:

- 2 wooden dowels, each about 20 centimetres long and at least 1 centimetre across
- 1 wooden dowel, 15 centimetres long and at least 0.5 centimetre across
- 1 cardboard tube (the inside of toilet roll or a thick-walled clothes de-hairing roll)
- 1 wooden tenon or a piece of cardboard as a bottom for the twiddling element.

Drill a vertical hole into the two thicker wooden dowels about 2 centimetres from the ends. The thinner dowel is threaded through this hole.

Drill two holes 1 centimetre deep and 10 centimetres apart into the 2-centimetre-thick board at the bottom. Fill the holes with wood glue and stick

Get the play action moving; for example with see-through turning tubes …

The trick with the twiddling tube is best demonstrated by a true professional. (Photo: Dbalý)

… and drawers made from matchboxes containing hidden treats. (Photos: Slawik)

The right board for every cat

the two wooden dowels inside so the two drill holes end up opposite each other. Thread the thin dowel through the two drill holes to align them parallel with each other.

With an awl, drill two holes opposite each other in the middle of the cardboard tube and glue the wooden stopper on to form the bottom. If everything has dried completely, pull out the horizontal dowel and hang up the tube. The tube must turn very easily.

Choose the modules for the fumbling board according to the games your cat is particularly fascinated by. Does your cat like hunting games, water games, smelling games, or are they the thinker and explorer of the family? If you know that your cat eats bits of cardboard, you should make the playing station entirely from wood.

You can guarantee interest by putting dried food in the receptacles on the fumbling board at feeding time. (Photo: Dbalý)

A good time for introducing the fumbling board to your cat is at feeding time. If you have not yet introduced fixed feeding times for your cat, you should wait until the cat is active and obviously in a mood for play. If your cat has access to dried cat food at all times, why don't you offer it to them on the fumbling board instead?Now the task in hand is to show your cat what you have prepared and how it works. Install the fumbling board so it can't slide, and begin to fill it with food. Most cats will come running full of curiosity, in order to see what novelty there is to be gawped at. In order to motivate your cat to get busy with the playing station from the start, it's best to offer them their absolutely most coveted treat or favourite toy of the day. Small treats or food that can easily be cut into many small pieces are suitable. These portions should as usual be counted as part of the cat's daily ration.

After the first fumbling efforts you can fill all the modules with these temptations. Make sure the treats are within easy reach of the cat. Later, when the cat scores good hunting successes and enjoys the fumbling, it will be more interesting if the modules are no longer filled to the brim. Some cats will use their claws and teeth in order to get to the treats. You can also block some of the openings with (rustling) paper. This seems to increase the enjoyment considerably.

Some cats develop such a great enthusiasm for fumbling that they will keenly dig out the treats, but they don't bother to eat them because they are too busy pawing for the next treat. Once cats have experienced how much they enjoy pawing for things, from time to time you can offer them less desirable treats for a change. To cats like these it's worth increasingly offering toys in suitable modules.

The paw, the perfect tool

Cats have extremely agile, touch sensitive paws that they use naturally for exploring their environment. Prey and unfamiliar toys are nudged before they are sniffed.

Cats who are allowed to hunt sometimes let their prey escape into cracks and crevices, just so they can fumble them out again with their paws.

It is not just the purposeful use of their paws that is innate to cats, but also looking for stimuli that trigger the pawing.

Pawing skills have to be honed too!
(Photo: Slawik)

At night, under cover of darkness, very timid cats can investigate the fumbling board undisturbed. (Photo: Slawik)

What to do with a scaredy cat?

Some, often elderly or anxious, cats will be too nervous to stick their paws inside any openings. Show them how it's done. Cats are excellent observers and mimics; as a result they are very good at learning through observation. Rather timid cats, however, can become even more inhibited by the presence of a human being who is possibly staring at them in anticipation as well.

Sit down a bit further away from a cat like this, and observe them discreetly and calmly from a distance. For a very anxious cat it is advisable to put up a simple fumbling board with fixed modules in a quiet corner of a room where the cat

is happy to be. Some cats feel more comfortable if the board is installed under a table or a chair. Before going to bed you can put particularly good treats in every module, making sure the cat can hear and see you doing it. Under cover of darkness your cat can explore and try out the fumbling oasis at their leisure. If the treats have gone by next morning, curiosity has overcome the cat's fear.

Other cats, on the other hand, are happy to fumble together with their human. From time to time, indulge your cat and fish out a treat for them. Watch as the cat learns something new each time – great fun for both parties.

Options for those not keen on tasty treats

If your cat does not like treats and also doesn't enjoy toys, there are other ways to make the fumbling board interesting. For cats such as these, modules with irresistible holes and crevices, in which things like feathers can be hidden, are particularly suitable. You can mount a see-through box with paw-sized holes above a bowl containing fresh kitty grass. A cat can stick their paws into the holes from all sides and from above and try to grab single blades of grass through one of the holes.

If you have several cats and one of them doesn't like treats, you can try the following: make a knot in a freshly picked blade of cat grass, pull it tight and cut off both the sticking out ends.

A fumbling board containing several grassy knots and treats will often entice cats who profess not to like treats and toys, and will keep even a very grouchy feline OAP occupied. New and reputedly very coveted scented toys can be deployed to maximum benefit here. If your cat avoids the board altogether, you should move it to a different location a couple of times. For many a sensitive cat the location is the deciding factor in whether a fumbling board will ever be used. Also, the materials used can emit smells that are unpleasant for cats. When a cat sniffs a fumbling board that doesn't smell right, you can clearly see them withdrawing and losing interest. Use different materials and build a new fumbling board. The glue you used may also be at the root of the 'wrong smell'. Offer a version of the fumbling board that has not had any glue used on it.

The cardboard fumbling board

Fumbling boards made from cardboard have the advantage that the material is easily available. They are quick and easy to make and you can use them to test which fumbling preferences your cat already has or will develop while using it.

The disadvantages are that they are difficult to clean, and they are more easily destroyed by cats,

Quick to make, but not particularly durable: a fumbling board made from cardboard. (Photo: Slawik)

First a wide ribbon is attached to the bottom of the cardboard box …

… then the cardboard tubes are put inside. (Photos: Slawik)

Horizontal tubes are well suited to beginners and offer loads of fumbling fun. (Photo: Slawik)

who don't go to work with kid gloves, than playing stations made from solid wood.

With a little effort, and even if you don't have a great talent for crafts, you can still build a simple fumbling board from cardboard. Inside a firm cardboard box the size of a shoe box, stack several cardboard tubes from inside toilet rolls on top and next to each other. If these tubes keep slipping, glue them to the cardboard box and to each other with a little wood glue. In order to prevent the cardboard box toppling over, you can cut two parallel slits several centimetres apart in the back of the box. Pull a wide ribbon through the slits and use it to tie the box filled with the cardboard tubes to a chair or table leg. A piece of string is less suitable, because it can easily cut through the cardboard. There you have your first fumbling board for cats.

For us humans there is a great temptation to put down the cardboard box with the holes pointing upwards. However, in the great outdoors, you'll rarely ever find vertical tubes with flat bottoms. For the fumbling novice it may be rather difficult to fish the treats out of vertical, tight cardboard tubes with as yet untutored paws. This is a task for advanced fumblers; beginners often don't have the confidence. At the beginning your cat needs easy to resolve tasks and quick successes in order to keep them happy and motivated. Of course there are also very boisterous cats who will pull out the cardboard tubes and continue playing with them on the floor. Let them have their fun – after all that's the whole point of a fumbling board!

Using a cardboard tube from inside a roll of kitchen paper that has been cut diagonally, you can let the treats roll into the horizontal tubes. This sound should make even a very lazy indoor cat finally aware of you and your construction.

How to avoid frustration!

Cats have a very short attention span and are very prone to getting frustrated. For this reason it is extremely important to offer easily available prey to fumbling board beginners. You can gauge if it is easy enough by the rate of success your cat is achieving with each fumbling attempt. If the success rate is too low, you should place the treats closer to the openings.

An interesting version of the fumbling board made from cardboard is the fumbling pyramid.

You need a firm piece of cardboard as a base, ten tubes from inside kitchen rolls, glue and a pair of scissors. Use a pair of rounded nail scissors to cut oval-shaped holes three to five centimetres in diameter into seven of the tubes. Begin with four adjacent tubes as a base, and glue the remaining tubes on top to form a pyramid. Put the tubes that have holes on the outside.

While the glue is drying, you can tie the pyramid together with a piece of string. Glue the finished pyramid to the cardboard base. The lingering smell of glue may easily cause offence to sensitive cats' noses and an impatient owner's new playing station may end·up being ignored with an air of disapproval. Leave the fruit of your labours to dry very thoroughly.

This playing station can be held in place by sticking the corners down with gaffer tape.

If you have a carpeted floor, you can put a chair on the board or squeeze the sides of the cardboard base under a table leg. Put treats into the tubes and let the fumbling fun begin.

Cats can be very impatient, and on occasion can treat the fumbling pyramid quite roughly. Some cats just enlarge the holes by pushing down on them with their paws. Others rip the tubes to shreds with their teeth and even use their claws in a frenzied attack, which gets them tired out really nicely. Let them. However, should your cat eat the cardboard, this is not a suitable material for your cat's playing station.

The wooden fumbling board

Fumbling boards made from wood have the advantage that they are durable and stable. They can be painted in any colours of your choice and varnished (please use non-toxic paints). This makes the playing stations washable and hygienic. Cats aren't able to destroy them as easily, they slide less because of their additional weight, and they don't have to be specially attached to stay in place. The modules cannot be glued into place; they have to be screwed down, which allows construction of durable, flexible modules. In particular, modules made from plastic can withstand rough treatment from a cat. If a module is broken, it can easily be replaced without having to build a new fumbling board from scratch.

The right location
Fumbling boards should not be put under scratching trees to avoid the cat falling on them and getting hurt. However, vertical fumbling boards can be attached to scratching trees.

Plato gets very excited by the holes in the fumbling pyramid – it hasn't got a base yet.
(Photo: Slawik)

The fumbling oasis

This fumbling board brings together various materials to form a permanent playing station.

Materials used:

- 🐾 1 wooden board, 2 centimetres thick, size: 30 x 40 centimetres
- 🐾 1 bamboo stick, 15 centimetres long, 4 centimetres diameter
- 🐾 4 white lids, 2 centimetres diameter
- 🐾 1 see-through spray can lid, 3 centimetres diameter
- 🐾 1 white yoghurt tub
- 🐾 1 see-through plastic cup
- 🐾 1 see-through plastic bowl from a ready meal
- 🐾 1 tube cut diagonally, 7 centimetres diameter
- 🐾 1 bottom section of a plastic bottle
- 🐾 1 blue plastic box from a children's game
- 🐾 several bottle corks.

First round off the edges of the board with sandpaper, paint the board with non-toxic paint and apply two coats of a suitable varnish. Then all plastic parts and the bamboo stick are screwed into place using short fat woodscrews. Suitable washers prevent tearing around the holes. Glue the diagonally cut tube and the corks into place with a hot glue gun.

Caution: sharp edges!

Thoroughly run your fingers over the completed fumbling board and the screwheads. Any sharp edges must be filed smooth. You should regularly run your fingers over a durable fumbling board in order to check that none of the modules are broken and all the screws are tight.

This wooden fumbling oasis is particularly durable. (Photo: Slawik)

The fumbling tower

Materials used:
- 1 wooden board, 2 centimetres thick, size: 30 x 40 centimetres
- 16 laundry balls
- 2 small traffic cones
- short fat screws and matching washers.

The fumbling tower is another easily constructed version of a fumbling board. The traffic cones are stacked on top of each other; the part of the inner-most traffic cone that sticks out at the bottom has to be cut off with a knife. This provides a better hold for the screws. First the reinforced traffic cones are screwed to the centre of the board.

Make a hole in the side of each laundry ball with an awl. If you thread large washers on to each screw, you can screw down five balls at the same level. Cross-slit screws are good for this, because you can push them into the hole you made earlier using the screwdriver as an extension of your hand. The next row of laundry balls is put above the row below, forming a diagonal pattern. Finally, one ball is attached to the tip of the traffic cone.

This tower forces the cats to exert themselves physically, because they have to stand on their hind legs in order to reach the higher cups.

Plato is conquering a fumbling tower made from laundry balls and traffic cones.
(Photo: Slawik)

*A wall-mounted fumbling board adds a bit of variety.
(Photo: Dbalý)*

Wall-mounted fumbling boards

Vertical playing stations can be attached to walls, doors or grilles and in scratching trees. You should make sure that a free-standing vertical fumbling board cannot topple over and scare the cat. The best method is to attach a vertical board to the middle of a large horizontal board using metal angle brackets. This stops it from tilting, and the cat standing on it provides additional weight.

An A-shaped fumbling board does not need additional stabilisers. Here the modules are attached to the angled sides. It's possible for several cats to play at the same time without getting in each other's way.

On vertical playing stations, flexible modules such as drawers made from matchboxes and tilting elements made from cardboard tubes can be mounted. Modules that require the cat to push down on something in order to receive a treat are also easy to put into practice. Glued-on letter cases are very suitable for this.

Modules for experts

Once your cat has gathered plenty of experience and fun using simple fumbling boards, you can create specific brain teasers for them. To prevent the cat from giving up in frustration, here too you have to make sure not to confront your cat with modules that are too difficult to fumble.

You can increase the level of difficulty of an existing module by making small modifications. The material offered is also of some importance. It's easier to fumble treats out of smooth containers than out of rough ones. Hard containers are more popular than soft ones. You can put this to the test using laundry balls, which are available in different materials. Mount a plastic egg box and a cardboard egg box on a board and see which material your cat can cope with well and which is more

See-through and flexible too: this module requires some practice! (Photo: Dbalý)

A fumbling box with plastic balls guarantees quick success with the treats.
(Photo: Dbalý)

of a problem. You can make deductions about other modules from this.

Many cats tend to give up easily when faced with games that are too difficult because they easily lose patience. Therefore it is important to attach one or two easy modules even to a fumbling board for experts. These enable cats to score a success even if they didn't manage to get a treat after several failed attempts; very important for a cat's sensitivities. Surprisingly, many cats really enjoy these brain teasers despite their tendency to get frustrated quickly; you should allow them this pleasure.

With tasks that require mental powers it is helpful to sit next to the cat and offer assistance where necessary. Seeing your purring housemate mutate into a little Einstein is very rewarding. Just like other individuals, including humans, cats have good days and bad days.

Even for cats who are fumbling experts and who enjoy mental acrobatics, you should have a second, less demanding fumbling board with only intermediate or easy modules, as well as the one that requires a high degree of fumbling skill. Fumbling boxes are very suitable for this.

A fixed module with an increased level of difficulty

The cat can easily fumble a treat out of a cardboard tube from a toilet roll that has been glued on to a board that forms a base. In order to increase the level of difficulty you can glue two additional tubes to the first tube to form extensions. The cat is now forced to stick their paws deeper into the tube in order to reach the treat. To increase the level of difficulty further, wrap the treat in some paper or cloth before putting it into the tube, and in addition block the openings with paper.

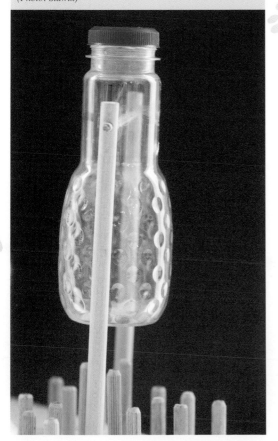

The rotating bottle is only suitable for very persistent fumbling experts. (Photo: Slawik)

A flexible module with an increased level of difficulty

For many cats the rotating tube (see page 95) is easy to use, depending on its material and size. In order to increase the level of difficulty you can offer the cat a see-through rotating bottle without a lid as soon as they have mastered the cardboard tube.

Once the cat has got the knack, and is able to empty the bottle purposefully without any problems, drill a hole a little smaller than the treats used next to the centre of the bottle lid. With the bottle screwed shut like this, a treat will only tumble out every now and again – the cat only receives random rewards.

This bottle is only suitable for very patient fumbling experts. When using dried cat food the cat derives added pleasure from listening to the sounds of the treats rattling inside the plastic bottle as it is being turned.

Inventor's spirit needed

Suitable items for fumbling boards for cats are durable, non-toxic materials that, after thorough cleaning, can be converted into modules. At home you can find suitable building blocks in every room. Even in the hall you can find firm cardboard tubes from inside de-hairing rollers for clothes. The kitchen offers cartons such as containers for tea, chocolates, rice and cornflakes, as well as the tubes from rolls of kitchen paper.

Many packaging materials for children's sweets (Kinder eggs, Smarties boxes) provide suitable building materials. The insides of chocolate boxes often contain useful compartments for

The flexible tower of modules is made from bottle lids.
(Photo: Slawik)

In the bathroom you'll find cardboard tubes from inside toilet rolls, tissue paper boxes, lids in various sizes, and even the balls from roll-on deodorants, to use for rummaging boxes. Hair ribbons and bands, which many cats like to take into their mouths and fetch, are ideally suited. They can serve as handles for lids on treat containers or for drawers that can be pulled out made from matchboxes.

You can use any bathroom pipe that the plumber may have left behind. Measuring cups and laundry balls for washing liquids out of the laundry room make great fumbling modules that are very popular with many cats.

The see-through cases of blank CDs from the study are also suitable. The paper strips from document shredders can be used as a filling for rummaging boxes.

The children's bedrooms also offer a wealth of materials, such as wooden blocks, wooden animals, large marbles for glueing down and various plastic toys that can be screwed into place. Dolls' wardrobes, with doors that have adapted handles, can be opened by cats' paws or mouths. You can even build a washable fumbling board for cats using Lego bricks.

Even in the bedroom you can find building blocks for modules. Curtain rings, curtain rods or their attachments, and cut-offs from curtains can be put to good use.

Nature holds excellent materials in store, such as rocks, branches, roots, snail shells, large seed capsules or bamboo pipes, coconut shells and shells from your last beach holiday. Dry leaves, large acorns, horse chestnuts or pine cones are excellent filling materials for rummaging boxes.

You can discover a lot of stuff in the garage, cellar or attic, which is just sitting there waiting to

tongue modules. In the fridge you'll find egg boxes, plastic bottles and their large lids, plastic bowls and yoghurt tubs, spray can lids and corks, which make good starting materials.

Faramir pulls a false bottom out of the bottle with the aid of a hair band.

Once the treat has dropped down, Faramir can fumble it out of the bottle opening.
(Photos: Slawik)

be adapted to provide fun and distraction to your cat. Garden centres, builders' merchants, arts and craft centres, flea markets and second-hand shops are also great treasure troves for versatile DIY materials.

No time for DIY?

Chocolate boxes, boxes of tissues, bricks with holes, egg boxes as well as letter cases are often used as simple fumbling boards. These present many cats with such a great challenge that they quickly lose their enthusiasm for fumbling after a few unsuccessful attempts.

The compartments inside chocolate boxes can only be reached by tongue – owing to their lack of experience many cats end up pawing the treat in vain. The shape and material of egg boxes also make fumbling things out of them difficult, and they are therefore not suitable for sensitive beginners. You can easily turn a box of tissues which only has an opening at the top – making it too difficult for novices – into an ideal fumbling box by cutting open the bottom corners with nail scissors.

For many cats the right angles and flat bottom of a letter case make it surprisingly difficult to fumble things out of. Horizontal fumbling cavities are better suited for providing success and therefore fun for your cat during their first clumsy fumbling attempts.

It is better, therefore, not to put a letter case on the floor, but instead to attach it with clamps to a table leg or a scratching tree. A brick with holes is best put down in such a way that the holes are horizontal.

Please bear in mind that a suitable first fumbling board has to be secured in such a way that it doesn't slip. You can quickly secure it by using a chair or a table leg, or some sticky tape.

Cat activity – the fun board

This commercially available fumbling board for cats was developed with cats of all breeds and age groups with any type of preference in mind. It is also suitable for cats with physical impairments. It can easily be cleaned, and it is stable and slide-proof on any surface.

Every module confronts the cat with a new task. You can fill the fun board with solid or with liquid treats, as well as with toys.

The fun board consists of five different module units:

- Ball module: Cats can do some target practice using this module. The see-through nature of the building elements makes the openings quite hard for cats to find. In addition it provides good exercise for increasing the flexibility of the cat's paws and claws. If the captured treats drop back into the ball, this creates a noise that the cat can listen out for. This way the cat can locate the treats with their sense of hearing as well. Toys can be offered as prey to be captured too.
- Pin module: This module involves locating the prey visually and developing strategies for fishing out the pieces using paws or claws.
- Multi-track module: With this module cats can capture prey even while lying down. This is particularly suitable for older cats and those with a low tolerance threshold. The prey can be reached easily and pulled out.
- Tongue module: This module is not suitable for offering toys. Using the tongue is the best way for the cat to capture hard or soft prey from the compartments. This requires patience and an

agile tongue. This is also an interesting play module for physically impaired or blind cats. Various treats in the separate compartments provide various smelling experiences.

- Tunnel module: Many cats find the 'mouse hole effect' offered by this module irresistible. They are very keen to probe inside with the entire length of their paw. This module is excellent for hiding wrapped up treats and toys. The cat can realise their passion for sneaking up on, ambushing and pouncing on prey. Captured treats are unwrapped outside the tunnel and used for further play action.

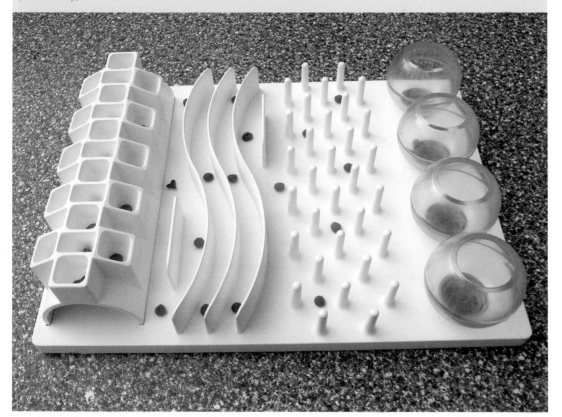

The fun board – a versatile commercially available fumbling board for cats. (Photo: Dbalý)

(Photo: Slawik)

Game over?

Nowadays we are often cautioned against the addictive nature of gaming. This certainly applies to cats' games – fortunately there are only positive side effects for you and your cat. The only risk worth noting can be the ambition some humans develop that can turn their cat's games and play into a serious business. Don't let it spoil your fun. Life is full of challenges and pressures. Enjoy this time with your cat and please always bear in mind that the speed with which your cat learns new games and tricks depends on their personality and preferences, but also on your ability as a teacher. We hope that your cat will enjoy the games presented in this book. We also hope that we have given you the impulse to develop your own games with your cat. The perfect game for all cats does not exist, not even in this book. Some games are indeed universally enjoyed by all cats, but at the same time there are just as many individual preferences as there are cats.

One thing can be said as a generalisation: there are no healthy cats who cannot be encouraged to enjoy at least some game. A cat who doesn't like to play is either sick or scared. If this is the case your first port of call should be the vet, who needs to check for any physical causes.

When dealing with an anxious cat you should first examine your own playing behaviour. Are you scaring your cat with noise or hectic movements? Are your children very boisterous? The roots of fear can also potentially be due to the cat's living conditions. Cats need more than just adequate space for running around and enough food in an urban flat. They are very complex creatures who need variety, tasks, a little education and above all attention to prevent them from becoming ill or depressed.

The very popular second cat does not always provide protection against boredom and loneliness. Many cats are indeed very sociable – but this does not always apply, and above all both cats should possess social skills, and the chemistry between the feline partners has to be compatible.

Between siblings this is quite likely; pairs of siblings of the same sex usually live in greater harmony with each other, because both cats often develop parallel play and social behaviours and will have similar needs and thresholds. If you have a pair of siblings of the opposite sex you should make sure you have the young tom castrated – and not only to avoid undesired offspring! At the age of a few months many tomcats develop increasingly rumbustious play and social behaviour, which can be increasingly scary for their sisters.

A compatible partner can offer an entirely different range of impulses to a sociable indoor cat than even the most committed human ever could. Please let yourself be guided by rational reasoning rather than your emotions when choosing a partner for your cat. The partner cat is above all supposed to appeal to your cat, not to you. As much as you may be taken in by a cute, shy female Persian, most probably she will not be a suitable playing partner for your three-year-old very active Siamese tom.

Now you have reached the end of this book of games, and you are hopefully at the starting point of a great playing career. We wish you and your cat a lot of fun in the process!

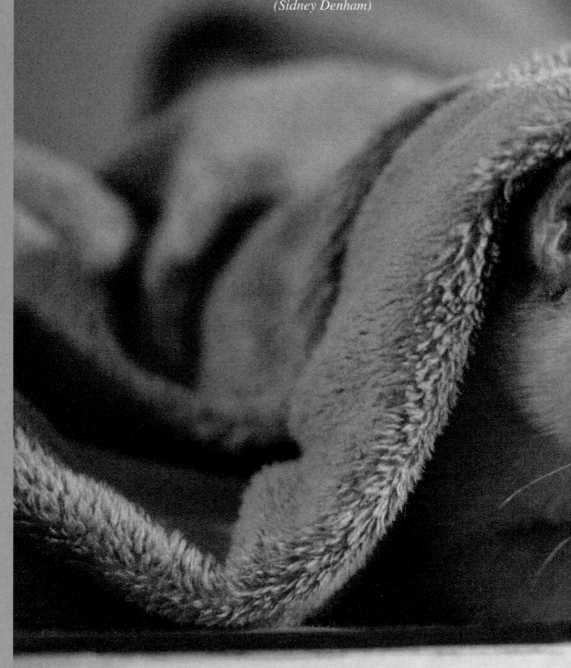

Cats don't go for a walk to
get somewhere, but to explore.

(Sidney Denham)

(Photo: Slawik)

Further reading

Chat to your Cat –
Lessons in Cat Conversation
By Martina Braun
Cadmos Books, 2009

Clicker Training for Clever Cats –
Learning can be fun!
By Martina Braun
Cadmos Books, 2009

(Photo: Slawik)

Index

CADMOS

GUIDES FOR CAT LOVERS

Martina Braun

Chat to your Cat – Lessons in cat conversation

Cat language is both complex and multi-faceted: cats do so much more than just miaow, hiss and purr! Find out what your little tiger is really saying with all his many different sounds, facial expressions, body posture and little behavioural quirks. Once you understand your cat better, you can get to grips with some of the typical problems and develop a closer bond to your moggy.

80 pages, fully illustrated in colour
Softcover
ISBN 978-3-86127-966-2

Martina Braun

Clicker Training for Clever Cats – Learning can be fun

Classical conditioning, used in a specific way in clicker training, is a method of learning, which no mammal is impervious to – not even the cat. Every click results in a positive reward: a treat, a cuddle, a favourite game. And because cats are intelligent, they quickly understand what kind of behaviour gets them a reward. This book gives you the chance to explore a new world together with your cat, from teaching small tricks to commands.

80 pages, fully illustrated in colour
Softcover
ISBN 978-3-86127-967-9

www.cadmos.co.uk

CADMOS